Evolution and Guilt

A THEOLOGY FOR ARTISANS OF A NEW HUMANITY

Volumes 1 to 5

The Community Called Church

Grace and the Human Condition

Our Idea of God

The Sacraments Today

Evolution and Guilt

ORBIS  BOOKS

VOLUME FIVE

Evolution and Guilt

BY JUAN LUIS SEGUNDO, S.J., IN COLLABORATION
WITH THE STAFF OF THE PETER FABER CENTER
IN MONTEVIDEO, URUGUAY
TRANSLATED BY JOHN DRURY

MARYKNOLL, NEW YORK

Abbreviations Used in This Volume

Denz. Denzinger-Schönmetzer, *Enchiridion Symbolorum*. Fribourg: Herder, 1963.

GBWW Great Books of the Western World, Chicago: Encyclopaedia Britannica, 1952. Volume 54; *The Major Works of Sigmund Freud.*

GS *Gaudium et spes*. Vatican II. Pastoral Constitution on the Church in the Modern World. December 7, 1965.

LG *Lumen gentium*. Vatican II. Dogmatic Constitution on the Church. November 21, 1964.

MED Second General Conference of Latin American Bishops (Medellín, Colombia, 1968). Official English edition edited by Louis Michael Colonnese, Latin American Division of the United States Catholic Conference, Washington, D.C.: *The Church in the Present-Day Transformation of Latin America in the Light of the Council*; Vol. I, Position Papers; Vol. II, Conclusions.

UR *Unitatis redintegratio*. Vatican II. Decree on Ecumenism. November 21, 1964.

Biblical citations are taken from The New English Bible, with the Apocrypha (New York and London: Oxford University Press, and Cambridge University Press, 1970).

Citations of conciliar documents, unless otherwise indicated, are taken from Walter M. Abbot, S.J. (ed.), *The Documents of Vatican II* (New York: Guild-America-Association, 1966).

Wherever possible, other church and papal documents are cited on the basis of translations in *The Pope Speaks* Magazine (Washington, D.C.).

ORIGINALLY PUBLISHED BY EDICIONES CARLOS LOHLÉ, BUENOS AIRES, 1972

COPYRIGHT © 1974, ORBIS BOOKS, MARYKNOLL, N.Y. 10545

LIBRARY OF CONGRESS CATALOG CARD NUMBER: 73-89054

ISBN SERIES 088344-480-1 VOLUME 088344-485-2

PAPER SERIES 088344-486-0 VOLUME 088344-491-7

MANUFACTURED IN THE UNITED STATES OF AMERICA

VOLUME FIVE

Contents

Evolution and Guilt

Is Grace a Social Reality?

Grace, the gift that God gives to man, has been the subject of an earlier volume in this series (Volume II). Using the terminology of Paul, we showed how the various dimensions of the human condition were transformed by Christ's "treasures," how they acquired new length and breadth and height and depth.

But what about these dimensions of human existence? Are they to be understood solely as dimensions of each human being *as an individual*? Is it a process that begins and ends with the individual, that has an impact on social structures as such only by virtue of an accumulation of individuals?[1]

Two weighty reasons would seem to militate in favor of a "yes" answer to these two questions. *First of all,* when Jesus himself spoke of God's action in man, he used the word *you* in such a way that it was directed to an individual person or else it intimated that its application to all stemmed from the fact that it was directed to each and every individual (see for example, Matt. 25:31). Jesus speaks very seldom of his Church. But when he does, he does not seem to have in mind any group impact as such. Rather, he seems to be envisioning the mode of action that each of the disciples will have to engage in after the paschal happenings.

Let us recall the image that Luke uses to report the Pentecost event to us. In describing how they were "filled with the Holy Spirit" he says that "tongues like flames of fire" rested *"on each one"* (Acts 2:3–4; our italics). A tongue of fire resting on *each one,* a wind that picks up *each one* and carries him to points unknown, a fountain of water welling up in *each one* and gushing toward eternal life, a bread of life that secures eternal life for *each one* that eats it: such are the metaphors used to describe God's gift.

The attitudes that are supposed to result from this gift either refer directly to God or else suggest a revitalized I-Thou relationship composed of sincere concern, mutual help, and gratuitous gestures of friendship. They lead to almsgiving, prayer, and fasting done in secret, for example. Prayer itself does not seem to derive its effectiveness from the number of those involved in it. To judge from the parables, its effectiveness seems to come from the persistence and confidence with which each individual prays.

At this point someone is quite likely to say that Jesus' way of talking about the gift of God is based on the predominant categories of his own time, and that his time was much less socialized than our own. In those days interpersonal relationships were decisive, some will say, and the guilt of a tyrant was always attributed to the tyrant *qua* individual rather than to the very structure of tyranny. If one maintains this, he will then be inclined to point out that the gospel must be translated into modern terms. Christ's talk about almsgiving refers to the payment of just income taxes today. His single reference to liberation has further implications today. Among other things it implies the abolition of the slavery that once existed, and of the innumerable enslavements that still exist or are being created today.

But this brings us to the second reason militating in favor of a "yes" answer to our original questions. The line of argument just alluded to appears to be a distortion of the gospel rather than a legitimate translation of it. In the first place life in the vast, complex, and highly structured Roman empire was not so centered around individual or small-group relationships.[2] Even way back then the tax system was a more decisive structure than was almsgiving. Jesus witnessed cruel abuses of power and had contact with slaves. In the second place, if one wants to transfer the teachings of Jesus to a supra-individual or social or political plane, then he must set up one societal structure over against another, one plan and project over against another. Yet where will he find such structures or plans in the gospel? Where are they to be even deduced from the gospel? How can he take this approach when the gospel seems to show a real lack of interest in such structures and even a marked relativization of them? Consider Jesus' response to the grave structural problem imbedded in the acceptance of tribute and the implied acceptance of the Roman social structure. If someone answers that problem merely by observing that the image of Caesar is on the coin, it seems that he would tackle the present-day problem of imperialism by remarking that the dollar is the decisive currency in all international transactions.

For this reason the Church is seen to have a "religious" purpose rather than a "social" or "political" purpose (GS 42); and in the religious realm it is the conversion of the individual heart that counts (GS 41). To be sure, when these individual conversions become a generalized thing, there is nothing to stop them from having a beneficent impact on the rest of society. The latter will benefit from the "reflected light" of God's grace (GS 40). Even the image of the Church as a *community* is felt to be necessary more as a reaction against the creation of mass man than as a reaction against the individualism evinced by Christians in their approach to the sacraments and the magisterium.

Now the weight of these two reasons is undeniable, and political use of them still continues. The most common form of this use is the notion of the distinction of planes and its consequences: Give to Caesar what is Caesar's and to God what is God's. In other words, let Caesar do what he pleases in his own terrain and hope that the conversion of each and every individual will eventually touch the heart of Caesar himself.

Here we might do well to ask ourselves whether these two arguments are compelling, even if we intend to offer only a preliminary answer. Actually this whole volume will seek to provide a theological basis for a negative answer to this question. Not only are the two reasons mentioned above not compelling, they are in fact erroneous.

Paradoxically enough the most important theological reason for affirming this is a dogma that seems to be out of fashion today. Worse still, in some cases it has led to an ideological justification of the status quo. It is the dogma that an *original sin* afflicts the human species.

Whatever opinion one may hold about it and whatever interpretation one may give it, here is something that is decisive on the one hand and structural on the other. We need only point to two aspects that the Council of Trent declared to be dogmas of the Catholic Church. (1) By itself original sin is enough to frustrate man's vocation, no matter what he may do or achieve in history (Denz. 793). (2) Original sin, as understood by the Church, is not simply the fact that each human being follows the bad example of his predecessors; it derives from the basic solidarity of each individual with all the children of men (Denz. 790). In short, it affects the very structure of humanity.

Without going into any further detail, we can say this: it is true that the most decisive happenings in the history of humanity have been an attack on man's collective structure and a redemption of this very same collective structure. We have these two events situated within the evolution of humanity, and we may well ask ourselves some questions. On the plane of revelation are these the only two events whose impact goes beyond the bounds of the individual? Did the structures created by each of these two events constitute the fixed framework within which each succeeding generation of individuals plays out its destiny in the drama of grace and sin? Are they the fixed poles between the summons of God and the response of each individual human being? Put in other words:

Are *sin* and *evolution* terms that operate on different levels of reality, the former being individual and the latter collective? Or are they components of one and the same single reality?

These are the questions we shall be concerned with in the following pages. Our comments in this volume, along with those in Volume II of this series, represent the basic outline of a *Christian moral theology*. The classical approach was a detailed exploration of the law, even when it began with introductory remarks on the primacy of love. Our approach here is quite different, but it is meant to form the Christian conscience in "the perfect law . . . that makes us free" (Jas. 1:25).

All the volumes of this series constitute a "*political* theology" by their very nature. But this volume in particular traces the main lines of what we would call a "theology of politics." In other words, it is the political version of a theology of grace, dealing with the gift of God coupled with man's effort in history.

NOTES TO INTRODUCTION

1. We gave the initial basis of a response to this question in Volume II, Chapter I, CLARIFICATION III.
2. See John McKenzie, *The Power and the Wisdom,* (Milwaukee: Bruce, 1965), pp. 4–7.

CHAPTER ONE

Evolution or Guilt?

In our present-day language we find two words whose interrelationships are far from clear. We talk frequently about "guilt," and if we are Christians we are even more inclined to talk about "sin." By the same token we also talk frequently about "evolution," referring not just to some restricted case but using the word in its broadest sense to cover the whole formation and duration of the earth and its present inhabitants.

The fact is that we often draw our everyday words from different realms and do not advert to the fact that their compatibility may be a problem. Where have we taken the word "guilt" from? We have taken it from a typically religious sphere, even though we may have lost sight of this origin. If we speak about "guilt" in connection with another human being, we do so because we have posited something of importance, something of the absolute in him; we see in him some trace of the primordial features of the deity. If this were not the case, we would use some other term besides guilt. We would talk about inconvenience, harmfulness, self-interest, opportunism, or some other term of that sort.

And where have we taken the word "evolution" from? We have taken it from the scientific sphere, where the existence of today's beings is seen to be the result of an inflexible, self-directed transformation full of suffering, death, and species extinction. The whole process seems to be something designed to serve our interests because we exist thanks to it.

This first attempt to juxtapose the two terms leaves us perplexed. Are they really compatible? Or do they simply indicate the superficial way in which we handle our basic vocabulary, without ever taking on the task of organizing its underlying content in a systematic way?

Section I

Let us engage in a little experiment that might shed some light on the matter. Let us set up a hypothetical case to see what happens when we take two professionals at the extremes and allow them to push their different languages to their logical conclusions. We are talking here about a distorted outlook, where logical consistency is pursued to the end while the rest of the world is left out of account.

In this case we have a professor of paleontology—or of biology in the broadest sense, if you prefer—on the one hand, and a professor of Christian moral theology on the other. Now let us suppose that we invite them to dialogue about the question that stands at the head of this chapter: evolution *or* guilt?

Undoubtedly the moral theologian, being a methodical intellectual, will begin by defining the terms being compared. He will tell us what he understands guilt or sin to be: i.e., a moral fault, a freely chosen transgression in which we disobey God and do evil. He will go on to say that man, by his very nature, is permanently confronted with a choice between opposites. He must choose between *a* which is good and *b* which is evil. The moral theologian will then go on to tell us that his whole moral science consists in the fact that it is possible for man to seek advice and figure out where *a* and *b* lie in a given option. When man chooses *b*, he chooses evil and therefore sins. He is guilty.

Listening to him, we must agree that this definition is correct. At least it is correct in the sense that it dovetails with what we have heard over and over again since our childhood, and with the notion we make use of when we talk about guilt not only in the religious realm but also by extension in the juridical sphere. And we may use the term in this way without even adverting consciously to it.

In all likelihood the moral theologian would add that he does not see how the hypothesis of evolution could possibly interject itself into the core of this decisive question about sin. We say "in all likelihood" because the fact is that the topic of evolution is absent from his treatises. Man will change. He will undergo transformations in many respects. His psychic structure and his social relationships will continue to evolve and become more complex. His store of knowledge will increase, thus bolstering his capacity to dominate nature. But insofar as sin is concerned, nothing will have changed. There will always remain the necessity of choosing and the possibility of choosing evil.

Morally speaking, man is made in a particular way once and for all. By virtue of this fact he is ever situated before the identical option between good and evil—no matter what changes he undergoes and what progress he makes. To sin or not to sin: this is something which history will never be able to change. No evolution will ever displace one of these two alternatives. No evolution will build up a facility for one or the other. We see this clearly in the evolution of each individual's life, which is a symbol and epitome of the universal process. The transformations take place on a plane that does not affect the decisive problem of the moral issue. Whether we are rich or poor, educated or illiterate, affluent or underdeveloped, we all are confronted with the same option between good and evil that faced our predecessors and will face our descendants.

Now let us turn to the other party in our hypothetical dialogue. Let us listen to a scientist who is concerned about the origin of life and its varied species. He may not begin by offering such a clearcut definition of evolution as the moral theologian did of sin. In fact our ability to define something human independently of its biological history will be the first thing he will call into question.

For the scientist a notion of sin that pictures man confronted with a constant choice between good and evil does not appear to conform to the facts. There are serious doubts that man is that ideally free, that evenly balanced between the positive and the negative. And these doubts apply even to today's human beings, who are the end result of millions of years of history. Does man even really know what is good and what is evil? Or are these terms that he applies to his actions afterwards, imagining that he is the master of these actions?

In other words this free will equally balanced between good and evil, of which the moral theologian speaks, will appear to be nothing more than an abstraction to the biologist. It bears little resemblance to a real human being of flesh and blood. For in the latter heredity, environment, and all the powerful influences from the unfathomable past form by far the most important and decisive part of that which man desires and carries out.

Man is not a finished, readymade concept. The word *man* designates a painfully slow process whereby the evolution of the animal kingdom gradually gives rise to a being which we are willing to call "man" only in a certain sense and only with great difficulty.[1] We are far from willing to admit into our company the beings which prehistoric science calls "human beings." We would be much more inclined to shun them and keep them out of our society, to regard them as creatures who have little or nothing in common with the beings who attend our schools, work in our factories, and are subject to our laws.

As the biologist sees it, then, one animal species is "being hominized" in the time that we call history as if it were the only true time, when in fact it is like all prior stages of time: i.e., a stage transmitted by the past and launched toward a future that is partly foreseeable and partly not foreseeable.

The "specialization" involved in this "arrow of evolution" consists in the development of a nervous system that is capable of systematizing the data of reality in a rational way. Thus what we call moral conscience is still in gestation even today. It is still emerging from its more primitive and instinctual forms; it is still unfolding in and through the tangle of instincts and determinisms which form the sure basis of homanization and which can never be totally abandoned. What is more, as the instincts and determinisms are abandoned or replaced, our natural security gives way to the unforeseeable and perhaps even to the catastrophic.

This has certain implications for the moral conscience. In very many cases what the moral conscience calls "good" is not within its reach. Even if it were within its power, it would not be its authentic "good." Instead it would be a dangerous ideal capable of unbalancing the ever unstable equilibrium which does propel us toward the future but only in very precise stages.

Listening to these words of the scientist, we again feel comfortable with the perspectives he has opened up. Even though his outlook is more novel than that of the moral theologian, it is already part of our everyday cultural baggage. No one thinks that man fell to earth like some meteorite. Our most common jokes, familiar to everyone, allude to our animal ancestry. We know how lost we feel when we read about a trial in which a jury is asked to decide the defendant's degree of responsibility. For the members of the jury are being asked to determine to what extent society can hold a human being to account for the use of his or her "liberty." We contemplate certain moral norms that are. acknowledged to be among the universal rights of man, and we ask ourselves uneasily whether they are really suitable for every country, every region, and every stage of development. An example would be those which provide for the establishment of democratic mechanisms. In short, we feel at home with the language of the scientist. Our familiarity with the idiom of the moral theologian does not prevent us from feeling at home with the language of the biologist as well. And yet the two are clearly opposed to each other.

What is more, this opposition deepens when the two interlocutors broach the problem of "evolution *or* guilt" in the distant past of the human race.

As far as the Christian is concerned at least, the moral theologian has kept a mighty ace up his sleeve. If it comes down to comparing the free will of the first human beings with our own, he will say that there has been no evolution from then to now at all; in fact there has been a blatant diminution that has been far from gradual. We today certainly do weigh moral goods and evils with our free will, and they do have a certain influence; but this influence extends only to us and a few other persons. By contrast the first human beings had all of humanity at their mercy, and the latter hung on their decision. What is more, the influence of their option was not just the "physical" influence that every human act exerts causally on those who are dependent on it. It was also a "moral" influence *converting every future human being into a sinner* with a tendency toward evil even before these beings had begun to exercise their own free will.

Our scientist would reply that these statements seem even more unlikely to him than the earlier ones. He would say that if the believer sees the plan of the Creator himself in the gradual gestation of the universe and man, then he must admit that no "sin" of such verifiable[2] magnitude could have interrupted the evolution of the human species.

If Adam was really the first human being, then the abundant data of paleontology puts him much closer to the present-day chimpanzee than to us. He was much more subjugated to his instincts that any evildoer, irresponsible by virtue of heredity, who appears before our courts. Modern psychological tests would undoubtedly classify him as a "congenital cretin." This does not judge him in terms of the tasks and responsibilities that faced him back then, but in terms of our present-day ideas of liberty and personal responsibility. Our scientist would add that only a magical outlook could regard the destiny of humanity as the proper object, and hence the outcome, of Adam's primitive willing. His task was a very different and much more humble one: to survive in the face of the immense dangers that lurked around him. Man's responsibility for families, groups, classes, nations, and international structures, which has finally reached the point where a small group of human beings have the capacity to annihilate life on this planet, is precisely one of the criteria that mark out the stages through which the human species has passed and reveals its tieup with the whole prior evolution of man. If you are a believer, the scientist would say, then you must see this as God's plan for creation as a whole. If you are not a believer, then you have one more reason for rejecting a distorted interpretation that is not only incomprehensible but also belied by all the known facts.

There we have our dialogue, or debate if you will. Only the setting and the characters are fictitious. The idioms and the arguments are certainly an authentic part of real history.

Section II

So we should not be too surprised to find that two of the most vigorous representatives of Catholicism in the middle of the twentieth century stood poles apart in their viewpoints, even though they did not reach the extremes typified above and evinced some vacillation. We refer to Romano Guardini and Pierre Teilhard de Chardin. Both had command of broad areas of human learning and science. Both wondered what the future could have in store for man's liberty. And both were sensitive to opposing viewpoints.

Let us begin with a key statement by Guardini:

> For Revelation, however, history's sense lies in the fulfillment of salvation. From God's point of view, salvation means that his will has fulfilled itself, and the predestined number of the elect is full; from man's viewpoint, that he has decided for or against Christ. This double process of God's "bringing home" the elect, soul by soul, and of man's essential decision one way or the other, continues progressively to the predetermined limits of time. When the fulness of time has been attained, the end will come. From the Christian standpoint then, all historical events have but one purpose: to clearly illustrate this decisive aspect. They are but constantly new situations in which it may be realized. If anything further on the subject of history can be said, then certainly not that during its course mankind grows better or worse, but that the object of the decision forced upon it is revealed with increasing clarity; that the option itself becomes increasingly inescapable, the force flung into the battle ever weightier, the Yes! or No! increasingly fundamental.[3]

In this passage we note a subtle blend of evolution and immobilism. If evolution does attain its end result, that does not matter one way or the other insofar as the essential is concerned. Good and evil, endowed with enormous proportions and never diminishing or prejudicing each other, will continue to contend for the free will of the individual right up to the end. At some quantitative limit, when some "number" has been reached, the contest will be declared over while the two adversaries still stand facing each other. To be sure, history does contribute something; the past is not exactly equivalent to the present, and the present is not exactly equivalent to the future. But it is indecision that increases, not the good. If that is what "hominization" consists of, then the final human being will be responsible for a good and an evil as huge as the world itself. But his responsibility, like that of all his predecessors, will be moral only. By giving his adherence to one of these two enormous forces he will not thereby give it victory—not even partial victory. If God were to prolong history still longer, his successors would still face the same option.

Even prescinding from faith we must admit that there is solid realism in this conception. Can parents spare their children the anguish of recommencing the adventure of the human species, whatever economic situation, education, or cultural heritage they may bequeath to them?

Can they spare them the task of playing out their liberty vis-à-vis the unknown? Does progress prevent unforeseen evils and new forms of egotism from surfacing in each and every epoch? In the light of our experience, can any of us say that the human beings of the World War II generation were born with "greater goodness" than those of the Stone Age?

It is more difficult to sum up the systematic thought of Teilhard de Chardin.[4] His impact was due precisely to the fact that he noticed the profound analogies existing between the conceptual elements used by the natural sciences—all of them being based on the hypothesis of a general evolution of the universe.

In favorable circumstances, according to him, a mere calculation of probabilities indicates that it is impossible for nature not to succeed in giving rise to a new, qualitatively different and superior synthesis in the course of an infinite number of trials and errors. This has proved to be a sure, inexorable, and overall orientation throughout the long journey from inorganic matter to man.

What happens when we get to man? "The statistical effect of a vast number of liberties is to diminish their chances of error and of losing the way. They take the right road. Nothing can prevent mankind from advancing towards its term; but the determinacy lies in super-liberty and not in infra-liberty [our comment: which is the case in the rest of evolution]."[5]

Or again: "The higher reflection rises and the more it builds up its strength (as a result of combined reflections) within the human mass, the more too, as an effect of organized vast numbers, do the chances of mistakes (both deliberate and involuntary) decrease in the noosphere."[6]

In this outlook it is evident that the passage of time does not leave our two moral antagonists intact with all their strength. Good and evil do not intensify their respective attacks. One of them, it seems, succumbs. Teilhard de Chardin sums it up clearly in a simple statement: "From the moment when men have woken to an explicit consciousness of the evolution that carries them along, and begin to fix their eyes, as one man, on one same thing ahead of them, by that very fact they must surely begin to love one another."[7]

It should not surprise us to find that Teilhard de Chardin was accused of systematically ignoring sin, or at least of minimizing it.[8] Perhaps the most well-informed comment about this comes from another theologian devoted to scientific work. Phillippe Roqueplo says:

> We are quite sure that Teilhard de Chardin was a man who was thrown into great anguish and almost total bewilderment by his contemplation of evil. We know that he was far from taking the living, saving presence of Christ

out of his spiritual life. So how do we explain this obvious deficiency, which clearly runs contrary to his intention? Let me suggest an answer that I feel has some importance . . . If Teilhard de Chardin did not really talk about the problem of evil and redemption, it was not because he was carried away by some sort of naive optimism and did not think about it or did not want to talk about it. *It was because he could not do it, despite his intention.* Why not? you ask. Because . . . his thought was organized around the modalities peculiar to a scientific schema and dealt with trajectory, convergence, structure, etc." [9]

With these words about Teilhard de Chardin, Roqueplo establishes once again the incompatibility of the two idioms we have been talking about: that which talks about evolution and that which talks about sin, the language of the biologist and the language of revelation concerning sin. But here again we feel divided. For who dreams of sparing his successors the task of choosing? What we manage to get from history is to bequeath better structures to those who will follow us. Yet we see in many instances that these new structures will entail unforeseen evils equivalent to those in the past. And does this not nullify the whole thrust of our struggle in history?

Let us stop here for a moment, pondering a disturbing and peculiar fact. We Christians, along with many other people, bring together elements from very different idioms to talk about our most critical and decisive problems. And sometimes these idioms are opposed if not downright contradictory.

Our conception of guilt is transmitted by an *immobilist* language, that is, a language which conceives the world and man as constituted once and for all in a particular way. By contrast the language of evolution may move from the nonhuman to the human with the same thought mechanisms that were verified in the former. If it does, it will conclude that guilt is nothing more than one of the infinite trials and errors that failed, nothing more than an inevitable and nontranscendent error in an ever-ascending march.

Are we once again faced with an either-or: science *or* faith, biology *or* revelation, evolution *or* guilt? Our hypothesis is that there is no such either-or confronting us, even though a correct synthesis is not an easy task. That is what we shall try to prove in the chapters that follow.

NOTES TO CHAPTER ONE

1. These difficulties have been conceived and portrayed very imaginatively in Vercors' work, *Les animaux dénaturés,* which served as the basis for the theatrical work *Zoo.*

2. At least in concupiscence, the concretely experienced result of the primordial sin.

3. Romano Guardini, *The Lord,* Eng. trans. by Elinor C. Briefs (Chicago: Regnery, 1954), pp. 512–513.

4. Henri de Lubac has shown that outside of his systematic work Teilhard de Chardin employed the language of sin and guilt as every other Christian does (see Henri de Lubac, *The Religion of Teilhard de Chardin,* Eng. trans. by René Hague, New York: Desclee, 1967). But the problem does not reside there. We have already seen that the dissociation of language within one and the same person is a sign of our age.

5. Lecture given in 1948, *Le Néo-humanisme et ses réactions sur le christianisme.* Cited in Emile Rideau, *The Thought of Teilhard de Chardin,* Eng. trans. by René Hague (New York: Harper & Row, 1967), p. 551.

6. *Man's Place in Nature,* p. 119. Cited in Rideau, *ibid.*

7. Rideau, *ibid.,* p. 54.

8. With his usual pedantry Maritain marvelled at the fact that Teilhard de Chardin did not have a solid familiarity with Thomism. If he had known and professed it, he would not have been Teilhard de Chardin.

9. Phillippe Roqueplo, *Expérience du monde: expérience de Dieu?* (Paris: Ed. du Cerf, 1968), I, 83–84.

CLARIFICATION

ECCLESIASTICAL ACTIVITY AND EVOLUTION

Our first chapter is an introductory one that merely attempts to pose the general problem. Thus it does not lend itself to CLARIFICATIONS that stress particular problems or aspects. Such particular problems will be discussed in the chapters that follow.

But it is not the general issue or problem that leaves us with a feeling of uneasiness after we have read the main article. It is the concrete examples we have used in it. In our hypothetical dialogue we presented an evolutionary scientist on the one hand and a *moral theologian* on the other hand. But the fact is that a moral theologian does not really represent the *overall* activity of the Church.

For this reason we shall re-examine the issue posed in this chapter by juxtaposing the evolutionary outlook alongside the present-day *pastoral* activity of the Church. The latter activity here refers to the Church's overall activity in the world.

The first thing we note about the Church's pastoral activity, particularly in Latin America where the Church should get right to the essential core of her task, is that the basis of practically all the Church's pastoral activity is parish activity.

It does not occur to many Christians that pastoral activity centered around a parish is only one of the many possible forms of ecclesial organization and life: that it does not go back to Christ or even as far as the primitive Church; that even if it did go back that far, it would still be a novelty amid a human race that goes back at least a million years. Even leaving that aside, why should today's Christian have to take account of situations that have been superseded since the institution of the Church?

Even more significant, however, is the fact that the agent responsible for pastoral activity does not deem it advisable to ponder this matter either. In general he simply feels that the *proper functioning* of a generalized institution, such as the parish is, is the proper guide and norm for pastoral reflection and activity. It does not occur to him to "relativize" the good embodied in such proper functioning; and here we

16

mean "relativize" in the good sense of the word. For whom is it good? He would simply answer: for everybody.

The assumption is that it is good for everybody to get involved actively in parochial life. The fact that many do not do this is deplored and ways of luring them in are thought up—for their good. The fact that there are stages in this process is admitted, but none of these stages is regarded as worthwhile in itself. It is something to be dropped as soon as it has served its purpose of facilitating incorporation into full parochial life. Human life is measured in terms of its approximation to full participation in parish life.

We use this example of parochial life for two simple reasons. Firstly, because it is the most general, basic, and stable institution of pastoral activity. Secondly, because for all its variations it is the clearest example of an institution which is valued for its own sake. Indeed it serves as a practical measuring rod of man's value; his worth is determined in terms of his distance from, or closeness to, this institution.

Now what would happen if we took this immobilist conception centered around routine and confronted it with the following principle enunciated by Freud: "Since a man does not have unlimited quantities of psychical energy, he has to accomplish his tasks by making an *expedient distribution* of his libido" (our italics).[1]

Some people may find it foolish or even scandalous to inject a dictum of Freud into a discussion of basic pastoral norms. But there is no folly or scandal in it at all. As we shall see in greater detail in Chapter II, the basis of any evolutionary conception with some depth to it is that the quantity of basic energy remains stable throughout evolution. The possibility of evolutionary advance does not reside in the impossible task of acquiring greater quantities of energy, but rather in the task of distributing this basic energy is such a way that better use is made of the latent energy that remains one and the same quantitatively.

One may disagree when Freud says that this fixed quantity of energy should be called "libido." Like commentators on Freud, one may debate what Freud himself meant exactly by this word. What cannot be denied is that "reason" and the "Christian outlook" are not something founded in a different source and totally alien to our instinctive life; that they are instead a different *distribution* of the same basic energy that manifests itself in our instinctive life; and that they *still* manifest themselves in it to a certain degree. The "economics" of energy require us to find out what quantity of energy can be siphoned off for deliberation and generosity, and what quantity of energy must be kept in the service of maintaining the instinctual part of our life. This calculation is not in itself egotistical. It is the foundation both of egotism and of effective self-giving in love.

For this reason we do well to follow up Freud's reflection here, as he opposes[2] the law of the (quantitative) conservation of energy with the Christian commandment:

The clue may be supplied by one of the ideal demands, as we have called them, of civilized society. It runs: "Thou shalt love thy neighbour as thyself." It is known throughout the world and is undoubtedly older than Christianity, which puts it forward as its proudest claim. Yet it is certainly not very old; even in historical times it was still strange to mankind. Let us adopt a naive attitude towards it, as though we were hearing it for the first time; we shall be unable then to suppress a feeling of surprise and bewilderment. Why should we do it? *What good will it do us?* But above all, how shall we achieve it? How can it be possible? My love is something valuable to me which I ought not to throw away *without reflection* (our italics).[3]

As the reader can see, the principle of the economy of energy is decisive here. But it is not meant to serve egotism. Perhaps without noting the contradiction in terms (neighbor–stranger), Freud presumes that I see before me someone who is a stranger—by virtue of his conduct (of which I disapprove), or by virtue of the fact that he does not belong to my circle of friends and relatives: "But if he is a stranger to me and if he cannot attract me by any worth of his own . . . it will be hard for me to love him. *Indeed I should be wrong to do so,* for my love is valued by all my own people as a sign of my *preferring* them, and it is an injustice to them if I put a stranger on a par with them" (our italics).[4]

In other words an immobilist moral "elevation"—that is, one which does not take account of the challenges we are forced to face with a constant quantity of energy—will paradoxically lead to what is in effect a moral decline. Why? Because compelling necessities will in the end impose themselves on us. If these necessities, which divide and defy men, are not overcome gradually, then any moralizing process will end up as its opposite: "The behaviour of human beings shows differences . . . So long as these undeniable differences have not been removed, obedience to *high ethical demands* entails damages to the aim of civilization, for it puts a positive premium on being bad" (our italics).[5]

It is worth pointing out that Freud, for all his criticism, does consider Christian love to be the supreme ethical principle. But he insists that certain conditions are presupposed before such high ethical principles can be effectively energized as love. If these preconditions are not met, then these ethical principles do not represent a *moral* precept at all. Instead they contribute to immorality by undermining the most elementary and basic conditions for real love.[6]

Now what about the pastoral activity of the Church? Its aim is to do as much as it can to instill, maintain, and foster what we might call "religion" or the "religious life" of people—to use a vague terminology. But two points should make us stop and think. First of all, the "religious" process around which pastoral activity is centered is not some vague or sporadic sentiment. As we have noted above, it embraces an ethical configuration of life that is very precise in its details and consequences. It entails sacramental and devotional practices, and it gradually introduces people to complex and definitive truths which define "orthodoxy" and separate some people from others both affectively and effectively. In other words, if we grant that man has at his disposal only a certain quantity of energy with which to respond to the challenges around him, then we must admit that our pastoral activity pushes him toward *a precise and determined* "distribution" of this energy without giving too much thought to the matter. And this distribution is decisive for the individual and for society.

Secondly, our pastoral activity proposes *one and the same* distribution of energy to everyone, quite independently of the concrete fields that must be confronted by the individual or society. This fact is certain, even though we may not be sure why it does this. For example, it may be because it considers the energy invested in the religious realm as the only supernatural kind; or it may be because it has an essentialist, static vision of the religious realm, compounded of minimal and maximal obligations.

Consider the doctrine of a life after death. If this is a truth revealed by God, then every human being would benefit by knowing it. But if a person accepts the existence of a life after death, how is he to distribute his human energy in the face of a given set of circumstances? Our pastoral activity does not concern itself with that question.

The peculiar thing is that God himself was concerned about the balanced evolution of the individual and his people in his work of revelation. He postponed revelation of the existence of life after death, for example, until a few decades before the birth of Christ. If the first important redactors of the Bible appear ten centuries before Christ, and if we consider this as the revealed word of God, then we will conclude that for ten centuries it would have been counterproductive for the chosen people to know and operate with the idea of an existence after death. And it is not difficult to see why. Read the Book of Wisdom and you will see the risk it might have entailed. In the words of Freud, it would have put a positive premium on being bad.[7]

The classic pastoral approach ignores this danger. One could say that the acceptance or nonacceptance of its demands, in terms of the human price that must be paid for them, is left to spontaneous regulation. Some accept them, some reject them. But this sort of "spontaneous regulation" cannot suffice. Why? First of all, because pastoral effort does not acknowledge this sort of regulation as such; it does not take it in its positive sense as something placed by God in the heart of the process of humanization. Secondly, because such "spontaneous regulation" does not preclude errors in calculation. For the most part the obligations are hallowed with the label "religious." Hence they are often accepted without conscious thought, even when they are suicidal for society. And this situation is reinforced by a pastoral outlook which does not recognize the danger entailed.

If the evolutionary vision of the universe is right, and if it is demonstrable that its rhythm is respected in the process of divine revelation itself, then pastoral activity must also take the mechanism of humanization into account. It cannot view it simply as a lesser evil. It must view it as intrinsic to its own function because the latter, far from escaping the evolutionary process, finds its own finality in it.

It is also our belief that this aspect of theology has special importance in Latin America. The growing chasm between rich and poor, the increasing exploitation of our national resources by the colonialism of the developed countries, and the growing sense of urgency concerning everything that has to do with liberation, all these things suggest that our pastoral activity must face up to this vital problem sympathetically and wholeheartedly.

NOTES

1. Sigmund Freud, *Civilization and Its Discontents,* Eng. trans. by James Strachey (New York: W. W. Norton & Company, 1962), p. 50.
2. An interesting example of the opposition between the language of moral theology and the language of evolution, to which we referred in the main article of this chapter.
3. Freud, *op. cit.,* p. 56.
4. *Ibid.,* pp. 56–57.
5. *Ibid.,* p. 58.
6. See a more detailed analysis of this in Chapter V, CLARIFICATION I.
7. Vatican II reminds us that "in Catholic teaching there exists an order or 'hierarchy' of truths, *since they vary in their relationship to the foundation of the Christian faith"* (UR 11; our italics). Was it referring simply to a logical, formal hierarchy? Or was it referring to a hierarchy pertaining to a harmonious evolution of man from the moment he discovers "the foundation of the Christian faith" to be necessary for his existence?

CHAPTER TWO

The Energy Basis of Guilt

Our general hypothesis is that no radical opposition exists between the language of evolution and the language of guilt. In line with this hypothesis our first task will be to point up possible analogies between conceptions that come to us from the natural sciences on the one hand and from Christian revelation on the other hand.

Roqueplo's comment in the last chapter indicated that the incompatibility lay in the fact that the data of science were framed from the viewpoint of *structure* rather than from the viewpoint of the individual. Teilhard de Chardin, for example, never denied the existence of personal sin. The difficulty with his thought came from the fact that he talked about "liberties operating statistically" in terms of the "law of large numbers." In this framework the individual cipher does not count. What counts is the total effect, the structure fashioned by an infinity of liberties operating in concerted effort.

If there is any analogy, it is precisely there that we must look for it.

Section I

What this means is that we must look for a negative structural tendency in the realm of those sciences which think in evolutionary terms. Only if we find such a tendency will we be able to establish a point of similarity, a bridge, between evolution and sin considered as a structure (and not in every individual case).

In fact this sort of analogy is nothing new. In our existing spiritual terminology we find terms that derive from physics, such terms as *inertia* and *gravity*. What is more these two terms are currently used as opposites of grace.[1]

As we shall see later, both are indeed valid analogies in the last analysis. But they do not fulfill the requirements we demand for establishing our bridge. Inertia does not say anything negative with respect to evolution because, in terms of physics, it is the tendency that bodies have in a vacuum to move in the same direction and with the same velocity as their initial impetus. Only insofar as it is opposed to *spontaneity*, to a being's capacity to generate its own movement, can inertia be set up in opposition to grace. And then we are no longer in the realm of physics.

Something similar is the case with "gravity." In physics it is the tendency of bodies to exert a power of attraction in direct proportion to their mass and in inverse proportion to the square of the distance between them. At least at first glance this does not seem to say anything negative with respect to evolution. Obviously enough this kind of complicity that exists between something inside us and an attraction coming from outside us can also metaphorically convey the motion of sin in us. For in this case the attraction of the things outside us is due not to their quality but to their weight and mass. But in using such metaphors we have again stepped outside the realm of physics. We have not yet found our bridge.

There is another principle of physics that can provide us with what we are looking for. It is the principle of the conservation of energy. Or, if you will, *entropy*. The principle of the conservation of energy is essential to any and all scientific thought of an evolutionary cast. It states simply that every natural transformation is effected with the same sum total of energy. *None of it is lost, and no new energy is introduced.*

This means, first of all, that evolution is effected by displacing energy, concentrating it, drawing it away from one function and putting it into another. When a steam locomotive is looking for energy to move from one place to another, no one and no thing provides it "gratuitously." Coal provides a source of energy that is released in combustion. The energy is converted into heat and ceases to exist as coal. This heat is transmitted to the water, the water is turned into steam, and the energy of this expanded water is transmitted to the gear mechanism to set the locomotive in motion. It keeps going until the fire goes out, the steam escapes, and the water ends. Then the locomotive stops.

This brings us to the second consequence of entropy. We said that energy is conserved. If this is true, then the energy that moved the locomotive must remain intact somewhere; and so it does. But where is it? If it is conserved, can it again be used to drive the locomotive?

The answer is no. The principle of the conservation of energy has its negative counterpart, and it is a serious matter. *Energy is conserved, but it is degraded.* In other words, all energy in operation is transformed into a simpler energy which becomes more diffiult to concentrate and to put at man's service again. In concrete terms it is converted into the most simple energy of all: heat. Strictly speaking, the heat is never lost; but it dissolves in icy space. Then it is like a wave in the ocean. Infinite as the sea is, we can assume that a wave always produces a displacement. But the enormous displacement of a wave at its point of origin is the source of powerful energy which can shift immense weights. When the wave is dispersed, however, this energy is dispersed into the infinite. It is not lost, but it becomes imperceptible. Once it is dispersed over many miles, man cannot use it to convey the smallest object.

Our example of a wave is not exact in terms of physics, but it will help us to "imagine" what this awesome physical reality signifies in the concrete. At the start energy is concentrated in some way. In operation it degenerates into an energy that remains constant but is simpler, more diffuse, and unusable.

The atomic bomb that released its energy over Hiroshima did not destroy any physical energy! It was converted into expansive power, heat, radioactivity. These energies expanded slowly without getting lost. They became "de-concentrated" and turned into innocuous energy that would never be usable again.

Thus once energy is released, it becomes more and more unavailable for future utilization. It reverts to simpler, more tenuous, and more diffuse expressions.

This brings us to the third characteristic of entropy, the one which is most important for us because it sets entropy directly in oppositon to the direction of evolution. Evolution moves toward ever more complex and potent concentrations of energy. But since energy tends toward degradation, as we have just seen, the work of concentrating it runs counter to the thrust of entropy; it is *negentropy*. So if evolution tends toward ever more concentrated and powerful syntheses of energy, then it does so by *running counter to the statistically greater tendency toward ever simpler sysntheses of degraded energy.* It is a minority current running against a majority tendency.

Putting it another way, we can say that every concentrated energy forms the apex of a pyramid whose base is the repetition of the simplest kind of energy. Take the case of setting a world record in some field of sports. This feat presupposes a calculus of probabilities into which enter millions and millions of failed attempts that are mediocre and fairly hopeless. One might say that strictly speaking the capability for establishing a world record can show up in any part. But if we are talking in statistical terms, then there is every indication that the record will occur where there is a real chance to make millions of unsuccessful attempts, not where there is a chance to make only a few attempts. Hence it is not a question of the survival of the fittest. The "fittest" is a community product produced by a multitude of less fit people who do in fact exercise their average capabilities and who thereby create the structure in which extraordinary capability is "normally" viable.

Thus living matter on this earth is very much in the minority as compared with physico-chemical bodies that are inorganic and simpler. By the same token the nervous system is an even smaller minority which is sustained by the infinite combinations of life that are more simple in nature. Life converted into thinking life is an even smaller minority. It is sustained by the energies inherent on all the other planes, but it is capable of concentrating and liberating energies that are dormant in them.

Above we noted that every new synthesis costs energy. The easiest synthesis will always be the one that is easy to come by, the one that is less rich and effective but immediately satisfying.

This holds true in the relationship between man and things, and it also holds true in relationships between human beings. The displacement of energies embodied in life on the human level makes man the most defenceless being of all. Man most of all is in need of a thoroughgoing education in order to confront the problems of living; thanks to the energy invested in their instincts, lower beings can solve these problems easily.

In other words man, more than any other being on our planet, is dependent on his peers; he is dependent on human *society*. The greater the development is in the human realm, the greater need there is for specialization of tasks. This entails a displacement of energies. There are some human beings who know how to do only one thing. In order to survive, they depend on the fact that society will defend what they know how to do and remunerate them with the necessities for life. They could not survive alone for long in the jungle, where more primitive people operate with relative ease.

What then is the spectacle we should picture to ourselves when we contemplate evolution, both before and after man's appearance on the scene? First of all, we see something structural at work. The individual—physical, biological, human—is an element that comes into play within evolution and in conjunction with it. The structure is formed by the fact that the larger quantity is dominated by a tendency toward facile syntheses—syntheses of a simple and spontaneous sort. If this majority is operative, relatively much smaller numbers of elements attain higher syntheses—syntheses that are richer and more concentrated combinations of energy. But that will go nowhere unless the latter syntheses transform the very base from which they started, turning what was "individual" chance in their own case into a more generalized state of affairs. Maintaining this delicate balance between majorities and minorities, evolution keeps passing new thresholds and moving toward higher forms of life and superior structures.

Section II

It would now seem that we have managed to establish our first bridgehead between the language of evolution and the language of guilt, between science oriented around structure and revelation proclaiming liberty.

Our reader may be surprised by that statement and ask us where we see a connecting link. This is a critical question. To answer it we must consider the peculiar nature of the analogy we are looking for. We have here two languages which, as we saw earlier, seem to be opposed to one another. But there is no question of their belonging to different realms or fields. If evolution is a fact, then it is a universal fact and the whole order of guilt is framed "within" it.

If we grant that, then we must also grant what Teilhard de Chardin says: "In the world, nothing could ever burst forth as final across the different thresholds successively traversed by evolution (however critical they may be) which has not already existed in an obscure and primordial way." [2] If evolution is universal, in other words, then all the energies or degradations we find on the human plane should have not just an analogy but an *analogy of continuity* with energies and degradations that are evident in other, more primitive states. If something we call guilt or sin does exist on the human plane, then, something not only similar but also preparatory to it should show up on the lower or prior planes. But obviously on those lower planes we will not find the feature that is peculiar to guilt on the human plane: i.e., an evil act done *with deliberation*.

On the other hand we do certainly find the following features: (a) a tendency toward the negation of evolution and its thrust; (b) a tendency to adopt the simplest and most immediate structure, to the detriment of other possible structures; (c) a tendency that is quantitatively victorious in the majority of cases, whether we are dealing with combinations relating to all individuals in general or to each one in particular; (d) a tendency that is not only overcome qualitatively but also utilized in the higher stages of evolution without losing its quantitative dominion.

Now do these features dovetail with anything related to sin, with anything *preparatory* to sin? In trying to answer that question we look at traditional theology and notice what it has to say about *concupiscence*. As a consequence of original sin, concupiscence forms part of the human *heritage.* It is not acquired by a voluntary act, it is received with the reality of being a human being. By definition it is a negative tendency that paves the way for sin, something that inclines us toward sin. Using another terminology, we could say that it is the involuntary structural sin of all that which precedes man, both outside and *inside* man.

Classical theology is not conceived or thought out in an evolutionary perspective. It does not say yes or no to any attempt to find an analogy between concupiscence and the first feature of entropy mentioned above: i.e., its opposition to the overall line of evolution. At least it does not offer a direct yes or no. But if the other features are verified, then we can offer our own answer to this question.

As far as the second feature of entropy is concerned, it is worth noting that traditional theology situates concupiscence, the tendency to evil, in what we today would call the domain of the instincts. Assuming that Christ was exempt from it, classical theology draws the conclusion that no instinct-based impulse surfaced in him, that reason dominated all his thinking and activity, and that his instincts obeyed this imperative and fully concurred. It is to the credit of Karl Rahner that he has shown that this view is in direct conflict with the gospel account.[3] But the point worth noting here is that concupiscence is unwittingly conceived in evolutionary terms. For it is conceived as the difficulty in translating the center of human energy from the instinctive realm to the rational realm: i.e., from simple syntheses to complex syntheses; from easy, mechanical concentrations of degraded energy to difficult concentrations of energy.

As far as the third feature of entropy is concerned, classical theology clearly indicates that we are dealing with a tendency that is quantitatively victorious, but it does not explore this datum. The realism with which theology views the fact of redemption is highly suggestive. By definition redemption liberates man from sin. But theology is careful to affirm that it does not liberate man from concupiscence. In theory this may seem very clear, but in practice it is not clearly known how the human species is liberated from sin when the law of minimum effort is operating in favor of degraded synthesis and the easy pathways of egotism. On the other hand theology has systematically rejected any and every attempt to picture redemption as a balancing factor whereby the good comes as easily to man as sin does—if not more easily.[4]

Perhaps the most interesting thing of all is to ascertain that the fourth feature of entropy finds its corresponding element in the theology of guilt. According to theology, concupiscence continues to be "quantitatively" dominant. But even though it speaks in immobilist terms about man's tendency to sin, the *event* that decided the victory of concupiscence (Adam's sin) is always characterized as the "happy fault" that merited for us the redeemer and his redemption. What else is this but an admission that the "quality" brought to the world by God's incarnation in history is immensely superior to the initial "guiltlessness"? Does it not acknowledge that man's tendency to evil, even though victorious quantitatively, is overcome qualitatively by man's new vocation; and that sin and its consequences were utilized to achieve a better destiny for *all* humanity?

Keeping these elements in mind, we can now return to the first feature of entropy and establish its relationship with sin. The tendency toward sin is the tendency toward the degeneration of energy which, of and by itself, would make all further evolution impossible. Of itself all sin is anti-evolutionary. St. 'stically speaking, we can say that on its own level "sin" has been all the easy syntheses that have taken place on the threshold of other new, better, and more complex syntheses that might have been. The fact that they are "redeemable" is no accident; it is a structural element, provided that the higher "gratuitous" syntheses do really take place. In the course of evolution prior to man that appears to be merely a game of chance, an indeterminacy. This indeterminacy is the prelude which paves the way for liberty. Once human history begins, this "grace" is given as such. It is a revealed fact, operating in a manner that truly is *gratuitous* even though it is not fortuitous.

Section III

From the preceding remarks we can conclude that the language of evolution and the language of sin are far from being opposed to each other. Indeed as their terms are refined, they turn out to be not only compatible but complementary. Only excessive compartmentalization can prevent the scientist from translating the mechanisms he recognizes in the biological sphere to the human sphere. Only a confusion between revelation on the one hand and its immobilist literary form on the other can prevent the theologian from making a complementary discovery: namely, if sin exists and operates on the human level, then it must assume more primitive forms in the whole process of universal evolution that leads toward man.

To terminate our first attempt at establishing a synthesis here, let us take a more concrete and detailed look at the obstacles on both sides which we have just mentioned.

One important fact about our culture is the strict compartmentalization of knowledge into separate disciplines despite the fact that evolutionary thought has become a generalized way of picturing the universe.

The scientist who studies those structures which link animal species in time finds himself without any instrument to ponder these same structures on the human level. Hence the political or social naieveté of so many natural scientists. They affirm evolution from animal to man; but they have no conceptual scheme for carrying this evolution further, for pondering the structural problems of human society, for examining evolution in terms of politics. Science, as pure science, becomes an excuse for political ingenuousness.

A very different sort of obstacle shows up in theological thought. Here we are not just referring to the limitations of the individualist emphasis which we mentioned in the Introduction. We are referring to something that seems to be closer to the very core of revelation. Divine revelation presents our present-day situation as the result of two *historical events* which, deriving from two operative liberties and from outside of evolution so to speak, determine our existence. These two events are Adam's sin and Christ's redemption.

One might accept everything we have said in this chapter so far, but then add the following: the two major events that determine what we human beings are do not proceed from a multitudinous, structural evolution but from two decisions in history. And to all appearances these two decisions were made with a force which does not proceed from evolution and which is inexplicable in terms of evolution, precisely because the degradations or concentrations of energy presumably deriving from this force are all out of proportion to the simplicity of the elements available on the evolutionary level at the time these decisions were made. It is as if one would be rash enough to claim that two monkeys rubbing stones together had released atomic energy.

So one must choose, and it is a choice that always cost Teilhard de Chardin dearly insofar as he was a theologian. Either one accepts the evolutionary principle and denies the possibility of such historical interventions from outside its orbit, or else one acknowledges such interventions as original sin and redemption and abandons evolutionary scientific thought.

The question for theology is this: Is the first alternative compatible with the data on Adam and Christ which has been so clearly revealed to us? At this stage of our inquiry the only thing we can say is that if we take into account the literary genre of the biblical authors, then such compatibility cannot be denied in principle.

An example may help us here. For many decades paleontologists looked for vestiges of a worldwide flood which, at some point in prehistory, had inundated and submerged the whole earth. Obviously these vestiges were not found, and cannot be. But increasing knowledge and familiarity with the literatures of the Mesopotamian region has enabled us to comprehend the technique that governed the redaction for this biblical narrative. In the light of real floods, probably in the plain between the Tigris and Euphrates rivers, a copious literature grew up. It depicted divine decisions to put an end to man and the earth, for reasons that were often capricious: e.g., because of the noise created by human beings.

It seems that the biblical author took over the already existing legend in order to give it a deeper religious content. The flood was a more just punishment. But above all it was the occasion for a pact between God and humanity. The earth would never be destroyed. After each storm the rainbow would reappear in the sky to remind human beings that they could cultivate the soil beneath their feet with confidence and in security.[5] As one can see, the event is disproportionate to the forces that supposedly were at work in it. But the author is not interested in whether the event did or did not take place. The truth which issues from the account is the comprehension of a given structural reality: the earth is solid and stable in God's plan and man can trust in it.

In like manner the narrative about Adam gives Paul a chance to explain the gap in man between liberty and its concrete realization. Not possessing an evolutionary outlook, which would not have been proper to his time, Paul gave an account of a reality and attributed it to a precise event, to the irruption of forces which we now know are far from possessing the power he attributes to them. Here again the immobilist outlook does not belong to revelation. It is its normal vehicle because none other exists. If all human beings are subject to sin, that cannot derive from God's direct will. The case must be that man himself, right from the start of the human race, is the cause of this situation. If the possibility of an evolution does not exist *in one's mind,* it is logical that Paul would rely on what the Bible says about the first man in order to explain what is now the very structure of every human being.

Can we say the same thing about redemption? At first sight the indisputable historical truth of Christ's life does not dovetail with an explanation such as the one above. In Christ we undoubtedly do have the irruption of a decisive happening at a specific moment in history. By the same token our faith tells us that it is Christ who introduced into man's destiny the unheard-of possibility of overcoming sin qualitatively and reaching God.

The problem here consists in attributing both things to the concrete historical *moment* of Jesus' life and death. Even the New Testament itself shows us a much more "structural" conception of redemption. Certainly the *message* of redemption bears a precise historical date. But the redemptive force pervades it all, both humanity and the universe. Hence the redeemer, as the creating, redeeming, recapitulating force, can be situated at the very beginning of all things: "He is the image of the invisible God; his is the primacy over all created things. In him everything in heaven and on earth was created . . . the whole universe has been created through him and for him. And he exists before everything . . . . Through him God chose to reconcile the whole universe to himself, making peace through the shedding of his blood upon the cross" (Col. 1:15–20).

Thus Christ has to do double duty in a line of thought that does not conceive the universe in an evolutionary form. His redemption must be simultaneously at one point in time and at the beginning of time itself. This doubling up is precisely what we will find every time we have to translate a profound immobilist thought into an evolutionary conception. It is our guarantee that the two languages are compatible.

But we will stop our reflection here for the moment. We have just presented two obstacles, and we claim that they are not irredeemable for the reasons outlined above. If we manage to overcome these two obstacles conceptually, then we will be in a position to move ahead. We will be in a position to explore in more positive terms the why and wherefore of sin insofar as it is viewed in the overall perspective of an evolving universe and an evolving human society.

NOTES TO CHAPTER TWO

1. There is, for example, Simone Weil's well-known work entitled *Gravity and Grace.*

2. Pierre Teilhard de Chardin, *The Phenomenon of Man,* Eng. trans. by Bernard Wall (New York: Harper & Row, 1959), p. 71.

3. See in this series Volume II, Chapter I, Section III of the main article.

4. *Ibid.,* Section II of the main article.

5. Gustave Lambert, "Il n'y aura plus jamais de déluge," in *Nouvelle Revue Théologique* 77 (1955) 581–601, 693–724. The title, alluding to the fact that there will never again be a flood, sums up the article well.

CLARIFICATIONS

I. FROM EROS TO LOVE

Freud may well provide us with one of the most instructive examples of the difficulty entailed in shifting, or trying to shift, from an immobilist perspective to one that is consistently evolutionary.

It is already traditional to point out three stages in the transformation of his thinking with regard to the content of the instinctive world and its impact on the totality of the human psyche. Freud himself alludes to three stages.[1] In broad outlines they may be described as follows. The first stage of his thinking, up to 1914, is marked by a sharp duality in the instincts. There are sexual instincts and ego instincts, the latter being instincts for preservation and self-defense. The second stage of his thinking unifies the whole instinctive realm, even the instincts for preservation, around the notion of *libido.*[2] The third stage is characterized by a new dualism,[3] but in this case it does not separate one set of instincts from another set of instincts. This dualism is something that pervades the whole life of the instincts and even the plane of consciousness. It is a struggle between two radically different tendencies or directions, Eros and Thanatos, love as a life-oriented force versus death or regression.[4]

These different stages do not abolish the continuity of Freud's thought even though they do lead to some ambiguities. But here we shall deal almost exclusively with the third stage for two reasons: (1) it is the most coherent, ambitious, and fully elaborated line of thought; (2) it is really the only one that affords an opportunity to explain, both ontogenetically (in terms of the individual) and phylogenetically (in terms of the species), how man has evolved from the psychic point of view.

Now in this conception the major fact for the human species is expressed succinctly by Freud in this sentence: "Our civilization is, generally speaking, founded on the suppression of instincts."[5] So we might well ask ourselves: What is the *force* that exercises this repression? What is its agent and whence comes its effectiveness?

In principle, three answers[6] might be given to these questions, and all three find support in what Freud has written.

The first answer would say that the instinctive sexual force would destroy itself in immediate satisfaction if it were not neutralized and converted into a force that is useful to society. For this repression society utilizes a part of the instinctive apparatus whose goal is opposed to that of the sexual impulses: namely, the aggressive instincts. When the latter are displaced from one's own ego and directed toward external objects, they lead to work and to the conquest of nature. But even this utilization of aggressiveness must take due account of that part of the instinctive apparatus which has been repressed (the latter retaining a certain preeminence throughout the development of Freud's thinking). It must provide time and opportunity for satisfying the erotic side, or sublimate it. It clearly does this in any and every culture, but the balance is heavily weighted in favor of aggressivness. So much so in fact that the resultant discontent ultimately threatens not only the free expression of instinctive Eros but also (and perhaps even more) the future of the culture. The fact is that the conscious barriers to aggressiveness are worth very little when compared with the only effective control over the destructive instincts: i.e., the sexual instincts.[7]

The second answer simply locates the cultural agent of instinct repression in something external: *reality*. Mere pleasure-seeking activity runs into the scarcity of the real world. Left to itself, instinct would wither in the face of "the frustration exacted by reality." [8] So at this point higher powers, powers that are more conscious than instinct, take over: "This *relation to the external world* is decisive for the *ego*. The ego has taken over the task of representing the external world for the id, and so of saving it; for the id, blindly striving to gratify its instincts in complete disregard of the superior strength of *outside forces*, could not otherwise escape annihilation" (our italics).[9] And we should take note of the very name Freud gives to the principle which now comes to the fore both in the life of the individual and of society. It is the *reality principle*. Operating through repression, it takes the place of the pleasure principle (i.e., the free, untrammelled activity of the instincts).

The third answer says that the force Eros, which is the only available energy in the whole psyche, can "be distributed" in very different ways. We are dealing here with a real "economic necessity" [10] and various possibilities are open to us. One possibility is to opt for quick and total satisfaction of the instincts, and the catastrophic result. The other possibility is the one which civilization chooses and which constitutes the very foundation of civilization. It uses the reasoning power of the ego to discern what is advantageous in a given instance even though this may mean witholding or sublimating satisfaction. The ego "dethrones the pleasure-principle, which exerts undisputed sway over the processes in the id, and substitutes for it the reality-principle, which promises greater security and greater success." [11] The reality which conditions satisfaction here is not so much something external as a pre-existing organization of

Eros itself. For it is Eros that keeps all the elements of a culture tied together, even though it is a desexualized form of Eros.[12]

In this case we are not dealing with some unknown "force" that frees itself from the pressure of Eros and permits it pleasure in man's spare time—provided that it will devote the rest of the time to disagreeable work. Something else is at work here. Civilization tries to displace erotic energy itself from direct sexual satisfaction and "aims at binding the members of the community together in a libidinal way as well . . . by relations of friendship." [13] To this end the *ego* must enter into play among the forces that do not cater to the direct, immediate satisfaction of individual instinct (and there is no instinct that is not individual). Only the norms of the *superego* permit it to distribute libido in a form that will be advantageous to society and civilization. But since only one energy exists, this submission to reality will in fact be submission to a reality resulting from a different distribution of the same unique force: Eros. In short "civilization is a process in the service of Eros, whose purpose is to combine single human individuals, and after that families, then races, peoples and nations, into one great unity, the unity of mankind. . . . The work of Eros is precisely this."[14]

Even though this third interpretation may be most in line with the final stage of Freud's thinking, it does not seem that he ever made a clear choice between these three possible ways of interpreting and explaining the repression that civilization exercises on the instincts.[15]

The important point for us here is to note that the first and second explanations are not evolutionary at bottom, for all their allusions to an evolution. The first interpretation, for example, pictures two divergent thrusts or directions (sexual instincts and defense instincts) on the same instinctive plane. It views them horizontally and it is therefore an immobilist line of thought like any other. The second interpretation looks more promising insofar as it establishes only one energy that can be displaced toward life (Eros) or toward death (Thanatos). But insofar as it sets over against this energy some "reality" or even "eternal" reality, it loses sight of the fact that a fully evolutionary conception would include this external "reality" within the process of evolution.

Hence we think that only the third interpretation corresponds in its entirety with an evolutionary outlook, and with the most profound levels of Freud's thought. Granting that, we may now ask: Are we dealing here with an evolution devoid of *sin*?

At first glance the answer would seem to be yes. At least that is the impression a Christian gets when he reads that the one and only energy—displaceable but identical—in the human psyche is what Freud at different times called *sexuality, libido, Eros.* Is he not justifying something that is regarded as "sin itself" by most Christians? And even if one is beyond that stereotype, does he not define sin as the opposite of Agape (love–charity)? And is not Agape the opposite of Eros?

It is with good reason that Marcuse writes: "The notion that Eros and Agape may after all be one and the same—not that Eros is Agape but that Agape is Eros—may sound strange after almost two thousand years of theology." [16] But in fact we must expand on this and say: after two thousand or more years of immobilist theology and immobilist ways of thinking.

If the forces we call "love," "charity," "Agape," on the human level do penetrate the lower levels of evolution—in attenuated, merely analogous forms—it is nevertheless clear that the instinctive level does not present us with anything in which we might be able to formally recognize "love" as the Christian understands it. But if it is Eros itself that leads the instinctive realm from the individual sphere to the sphere of groups and society, as Freud's thought asserts, then must we not conclude that Agape is Eros turned human, Eros freely shouldered by a being who is not only the object but also the subject and author of evolution on its own proper level? At the very least we can say that this analogy is clearly present in Freud's concept of Eros.[17]

We must likewise say that sin is present at the instinctive level as Thanatos, and this is fundamentally in agreement with Paul's thought. Sin is present as death, as regression to a state without suffering, as the rejection of new, unforeseen possibilities offered by reality.

As far as we can tell, it is true that Freud only speaks of the *feeling of guilt* on the instinctive plane, and of *moral good or evil* on the external plane. He sees the latter as norms imposed on the individual by a culture, which communicates laws to him from without. Nevertheless the consequences of his thought go much further.[18]

If the life-supporting forces of Eros lead to the adoption of an increasingly organized and universal reality, then the progress in this direction is not and cannot be in a surefooted, straight-line direction. In the more complex—more civilized—forms of Eros, the ego is presented with a set of conditioning circumstances which it must accept whether it wants to or not. This is what Freud calls the *superego*. In it lie the most universal potentialities of Eros, but also its greatest danger. In interiorizing the prescriptions of the superego and turning them into something instinctive, man can succumb to the regressive, conservative tendency that is part and parcel of everything instinctive. The search for a pleasurable adaptation devoid of conflict can be the search for a new maternal womb, for a simplification that represents a retreat to the inorganic level. In this case the inorganic would obviously be dressed up in human forms, because the species does not return to the animal level biologically. These forms would be mass-oriented forms wherein the conservative pull of instinct would take possession of communal and social forms that had apparently been wrested from its control. Thus the ambiguity of the word *love* (Eros and Agape) does not result from the equivocal nature of a tired language. It springs from the very same soil that is the source of its highest potentialities.[19]

The word *death* is rich with the same equivocation. To submerge oneself in the instinctive realm is to head for death. But the same fate awaits the person who leaves the instinctive realm and meekly adopts the established norms. The acceptance of the societal superego without reflection and personal checking is instinctive too. It too leads to death.

Not surprisingly then, this conception dovetails with what Schoonenberg has to say about sin: "The singular *he hamartia,* 'the sin,' acquires an increasingly special meaning as the tradition of the New Testament progresses. 'The sin' is seen as belonging more to the inner man than 'the sins' or 'the transgressions'; it becomes also a power which *rules over the whole of mankind*" (our italics).[20] And Schoonenberg adds: "That is why sin is not only the unwillingness to accept ready-made norms but also the refusal to help in *building and establishing norms. . . .* In this way sin is also opposed to the meaning of history. . . . Sin, although standing in history . . . is antihistorical" (our italics).[21]

Freud had difficulty in shifting outright to an evolutionary perspective. Perhaps we can say that his difficulty lay in a strain of *individualism,* whose parallel in the religious field we shall study in the next chapter. Such individualism was in any case inherent in his continuing psychoanalytic activity. Freud himself openly expresses his dissatisfaction with a work like *Civilization and Its Discontents,* a work in which he turned his intuitions directly to the social structure.

II. A SOCIOLOGY OF MASSES OR A SOCIOLOGY OF SIN?

Today much is written and said about the "masses." We hear talk about mass society, mass rebellion, mass communications, mass culture, and mass man. The masses are to be mobilized so that they can win back their rights, and we must develop a pastoral approach to the "masses."

However ambiguous the term *masses* may be, we all realize in some vague way that the "masses" are playing a decisive role in the evolutionary process, in the process of "hominization." Depending on the outlook and interests of a given individual, this role will be viewed as negative, or positive, or merely potential.

Here[22] we do not intend to decide the latter issue. We are simply going to clarify the terms of the problematic and relate them to the problem of evolution and guilt, viewing them as the decisive factors that they are on the human level.

If we are to judge by the various terms set up in opposition to it by different authors, the term *mass* can be qualified by the most diametrically opposed adjectives. It can be a potential for liberty or a potential for totalitarianism, a factor fostering revolution or a factor fostering conformity, a majority in rebellion or a majority under subjugation.

To orientate ourselves a bit, let us start from the *sociological* plane. However different and even opposed the interpretations or evaluations of the term *mass* may be, on the plane of sociology this term is always related to majorities that can be established statistically. "Mass" means a large multitude as opposed to minorities.

But if sociology is a science with verifiable hypotheses rather than

mere statistical compilation, it is so precisely because a majority translates into some kind of uniformity. Over against this uniformity what is
different is a minority. That is the first point.

To speak about masses in a sociological sense, then, is to speak about
a majority resemblance. Thus if one takes as his basis a person's social
status, that is, his place in the social scale of goods and services, the
masses are those who *at the same time* share a similar status and are a
majority. The aristocracy shares a similar status but it is practically never
a majority. For this reason it is not called a mass in sociology. By contrast
the proletariat would be synonymous with mass in certain situations of
urbanization and industrial revolution. Hence the association between
masses and proletariat, which is very evident in Marxist sociology. But in
a given society it may also happen that the middle class is the majority
and the most homogeneous group, in which case sociology would use the
term *mass* to refer to this sector of the population rather than to the
proletariat. Many works of North American sociology must be interpreted in this sense, to indicate just one example.

Clearly, then, the term *mass* is not employed to designate any special
social class—the lower class, for example—but rather to designate a majority likeness in social status within a given society.

Let's go one step further. Sociology always talks about "masses" in
opposition to minorities. Now one can talk about all sorts of minorities:
executives, Jehovah's Witnesses, migrant laborers, blacks, the super-rich,
etc. But in common usage the term *mass* is not applied to the majority
merely because it is the majority. We talk about the "black minority" for
example, but we do not talk about the "white masses."

Over against the mass sociology sets minorities which not only are
"different" but also have *decision-making power* over the majority. This
comes down to saying that on some planes and in some matters there are
people who decide for the rest in a given society. This concept of mass
and minority is the one wielded by both empirical American sociology
and Marxist sociology.

The latter typically views the masses as the exploited sectors of the
population, who are at the mercy of decisions that rob them of their
work and its products. Obviously enough the masses, still under exploitation, *normally* lack decision-making power vis-à-vis the dominant
minority. They must be mobilized, not so much so that they can become
normal centers of decision-making but rather so that in some extraordinary way they may decide to change the status quo that is exploiting
them. This in turn calls for a "vanguard." And this mobilizing vanguard
is once again a minority endowed with decision-making power, even
though its power is opposed to that of the minority now holding power.
The "party" is seen as this vanguard. After the revolution this minority
will replace the previous exploiting minority (as long as the role of the
State endures at least).[23]

This prompts us to take another step. There would be no possibility of structuring a science of sociology if the majority affected by the decisions of a minority were accidental, that is to say, if the group making decisions were to change from day to day so that there was a constant change in the majority who accepted these decisions. Sociology as a science is possible because the majority of which we are speaking is one that remains constant to a certain extent. It is not a fortuitous majority. The very fact and reality of its being a majority is based on some determinism.

In other words, there is something in the majority that disposes it to accept *the decisions*—of different sorts and unpredictable to a certain extent—of the minority. And the latter in turn possesses mechanisms to induce acceptance of *its decisions*, acceptance of its power to chose A over B and C over D.

Sociology formulates hypotheses about this determinism and then verifies them. It explores how far it reaches, under what circumstances a decision is accepted, what elements go to make up this decision-making power, and what elements go to make up the receptivity of the majority to a decision that has been reached. It also explores when and under what circumstances this mechanism does not work and the mass can follow another minority or breed its own potential leaders.

Putting it another way, we can say that sociology of itself is not the science of predicting what decisions are going to be reached by the minority. The latter is assumed to be *free*, and hence it lies outside the science of social organization. Sociology exists for the simple reason that masses exist: that is, for the simple reason that there are majorities who do not formally make use of their liberty even though they are potentially free.

Let us take a further step, however. Sociology does also concern itself with the minorities who have decision-making power in society. What is more, it can formulate and verify hypotheses about the nature of the decisions that such a minority group will adopt. On the other hand it must back off from predicting other things: e.g., What will be the matrimonial procedure of a couple, who do not seem to have any decision-making power in the social arena?

What does this tell us? It tells us that what is called "decision-making power" implies liberty on one plane only: e.g., the power to decide about some law or to impose some commercial product. On another plane this decision-making power can be subject to *another mechanism:* e.g., prestige, money, etc. To this extent, then, the decision-making power is not a matter of chance. It goes to make up majority forms of conduct that are constant and subject to statistical confirmation. For example, a statesman can have a multitude of citizens subject to his political decisions while he himself is subject to the group that dictates musical taste. More close to home, he can be subject to what older psychology called "passions" (i.e., passivities), and thereby find himself among the multitude which he rules on another plane.

Thus the "liberty" to make decisions, which belongs to sociopolitical minorities, does not disqualify sociology from formulating hypotheses and verifying them statistically. But why not? Because majority or mass-based mechanisms are operative within these groups who are minorities in terms of social *status*. "Mass" or "minority" is not due to external decree, or even less to social position, or to the internal makeup of a certain group of human beings. "Mass man" is the person who, whatever his social position may be, delegates his power of judgment and decision to others *in any given area or aspect of his existence.*

It goes without saying that there are areas where decisions evade the structural majority: e.g., those that depend on specialized scientific knowledge. But there are also decisions, even global ones, which never wholly escape free decision-making if each person makes the effort to shoulder decision-making power for himself.

With that, however, we leave the domain of sociology. It showed us that verifiable constants exist because and insofar as majorities exist—majorities with homogeneous lines of conduct resulting from decisions made by minorites. It also showed us that sociology itself is silent in the face of a decision that is truly free, for such a decision is, by its very nature, not subject to statistical verification and prediction. Finally it showed us that no one belongs structurally and completely to either majorities and minorities; that in the last analysis it depends on whether potentially free decisions are shouldered as such on any given level.

These suppositions, without which no science of sociology would exist, direct our attention to a deeper and more universal level than that of sociological science itself. Right off they tell us that sociology is based on the prevailing *entropy* in human lines of conduct. The thrust of minimum effort is toward simplistic, mechanical syntheses. Liberty is an effort and hence is essentially a minority thrust.

Starting from there, we can say that the whole process of universal evolution finds its corresponding analogies and its corresponding ambiguities. "Mass man," whatever social class he may be in, represents two things in the face of any possibility for new social syntheses of a richer sort. On the one hand he is a *brake* operating against such synthesis because the statistical laws of least effort are operative in him. On the other hand he is the indispensable *base* of solidarity required so that societal life may exist at all and so that out of this base the possibility of new syntheses may rise through the work of minorities.

We can put this another way that might seem odd in the field of theology. We can say that the human mass is *sin*. At the human level there is always an element of volition intermingled with the degradation of energy. It is the rejection of a creative but costly liberty. More precisely as sin, it is the statistical law that dominates the world and that permits it to escape the realm of statistics and find new, superior syntheses based on love without shattering into a million pieces.[24]

At bottom all solidarity is grounded on the fact that originality, unforeseen decisions, and the unknown depths of each liberty are minority realities. I can understand the sentiments and needs of my peers, I can instinctively exercise the "social engineering" of which sociology speaks in scientific terms. I share the prejudices of my group or my nation. And I share them because I do not try to get to know strangers, competitors, or enemies outside in a deep and unprejudiced way.[25]

The dictum runs: "Charity begins at home." It is the enunciation of a basic solidarity without which a group, a society, or even the world would fall to pieces. At the same time it is the enunciation of a sin, denying understanding, love, and aid to those outside and inculcating favoritism toward those close to me and, in the last analysis, a part of myself.

The basic danger facing any authentic evolutionary outlook is that it may overlook and ignore the two-edged—dialectical—role of the mass. It may turn it into an evolutionary determinism, passively waiting for evolution to spring from the bedrock in it that is actually more grounded on basic, numerical features. Marx put the Hegelian dialectic "back on its feet again" by giving it an active stress that it had not possessed. But he did not avoid ambiguity entirely, and what we might call an "economic determinism" based on mass reactions can appeal to him for support.

III. HUMAN RIGHTS: FOR OR AGAINST MAN?

An evolutionary outlook clearly makes us uncomfortable, disturbing our positions not only in the psychic and social realms but also in the *political* realm. Denying the ambiguity of reality may be comfortable and convenient. It may even correspond to some ideal we judge to be eternal. But the fact is that this "eternal" ideal may, unbeknownst to us, be gradually turning into something exactly the opposite.

Let us consider an example that is fairly worldwide. When the world emerged from the brutality of World War II, it seemed on the verge of entering an era where right would supplant violence. Democracy was restored in "totalitarian" countries, and the newly formed United Nations set about the task of working up a charter of basic human rights for the first time in human history.

But a quarter of a century after the proclamation of human rights we find that violence reigns in the vast majority of the underdeveloped countries. Violence and repression, the two sides in conflict, have refined their methods and proceed apace outside the framework of human rights. Is this due to man's forgetfulness, or to his wickedness? Let us take a closer look at the facts.

When the Declaration of the Rights of Man was promulgated a little over twenty years ago, only a small portion of this planet had a sufficient supply of goods and a social structure that permitted these prerogatives to prevail as *rights*. In other words they were human *values* for all, but real *rights* for only very few.

"Value" indicates a goal to be arrived at. "Right" indicates a basic minimum from which to start. For a value to be truly a right, it must be abundant and well distributed in a population or a society.

This is true not only of the social stratification within a given society (e.g., in a Latin American country) but also of the stratification of nations throughout the world (i.e., the imbalance and degree of flexibility between rich and poor nations).

For example, it is obvious that democracy is not achieved by exercising the right to vote. Democracy is a quality that precedes the voting. Voting ten or a hundred or a thousand times will not make people respect elections when the classes in power systematically vitiate them. The same holds true on the international plane. The citizens of an underdeveloped country may vote "democratically." But if the power of extranational wealth is so great that the major political decisions are made in the light of orientations coming from those countries which dominate the world market, then the *right* of voting democratically will not bring real democracy to a country no matter how often it is exercised.

So caution is in order here for those nations that are subject to great disproportions in wealth—either internally or with respect to affluent societies abroad. First of all, they must not confuse human *values* (which are to be sought after) with human *rights* (i.e., a specific panoply of *instruments* that are supposedly useful in obtaining these values). Indeed the confusion between rights and values here is not simply a matter of error.

In countries where human values are not distributed equitably, and in international groupings where the same is true, the dominant class or nation declares its own values to be *rights*. It does not do this because it is willing to distribute them to others. On the contrary, it does so because it possesses these values and also the means of controlling the operative mechanisms of justice (which could vindicate the rights of others and ensure their proper distribution). As a result the fight for these values is waged *in an atmospher where it is doomed to failure from the start*. To believe that the poor nations need merely invoke the shibboleth of human rights is to succumb to a costly naieveté.

Suppose justice is bought with money in a given country, and an innocent person is being hunted for a crime against some powerful individual or group. Some people might say: *Give yourself up and the law will vindicate your rights*. But if the person is not a fool, he will realize that in such circumstances no real right or justice exists. The proposal is a trap. If this person really wants this *value* "justice," he must look for it *outside of lawful rights*.

This does not hold true solely on the level of the individual. A film entitled *The Man Who Shot Liberty Valence* depicts the struggle entailed in shifting from a system of justice (or injustice) based on *force* to a system of justice based on *law*. And the thing that permits this shift in the movie is the *last shot* fired on behalf of justice and law but not "in accordance with the law." If the people involved had trusted in the law itself instead of this shot, injustice and the law of force would have continued to reign as before.

So far we have set up a contrast between *values* and *rights*. And we have indicated that the latter often are not adequate instruments for attaining the former. The next step would be to point out what other instruments remain, outside of law and right, for achieving these values.

It would be overstating the case to focus solely on violence—on armed violence at least. Any and every form of pressure, within the legal order or outside it, which compels people to distribute human values equitably is such an instrument. Their common coefficient is the discomfort they cause to the classes or countries that hold these values and proclaim these rights.

So the inhabitant of an affluent society is faced with a fundamental question as he observes the course of events in impoverished countries. Will he be capable of recognizing a quest for the same values that he recognizes and in part enjoys as rights in the increasingly systematic *refusal* of the underdeveloped countries to seek them *through the law*?

As I see it, this is the greatest cultural and Christian challenge facing any industrially developed country where human *values* are in practice equated with human *rights*. When it looks at the Latin American scene, will it be able to recognize and acknowledge that its only true allies are those who in fact do not respect or utilize or for the moment admit the standing of such "rights"?

We are faced with a big question mark when we look at our so-called "Christian values." Are they values well on the way to effective realization in the concrete? Or, insofar as they have been turned into part of the legal system and the established order, will they prove to be a barrier to the effective realization of the very order they claim to defend? And will they make it all the harder to see that there is a barrier to be overcome?

These reflections indicate that secularized Western society unwittingly continues to have recourse to what Christian theology called the "world of the supernatural." How else can we describe those human rights which come from an ideal heaven and for which social reality is merely a necessary support? The a-temporal *verticality* of these rights is the same verticality that some would force on the Church when they accuse her of *horizontalism*: i.e., of abandoning the a-temporal divine in order to subject herself to the conditions of history.

IV. THE EQUIVOCACY OF THE LAW

The moral law recognized by Western man is a secularized version of the "Christian" law. It may be broader or narrower, but no serious attempt has been made to create another "law" deriving from different principles.

It is quite another matter to determine whether this so-called "Christian" law—and its secularized version—really dovetails with the fonts of gospel thinking. When we see the univocal way in which people talk about the law in present-day Christian morality, it is interesting to discover the language difficulties that Paul encountered in speaking about the law and its history. It is also interesting to note that Paul describes the vicissitudes of the law both *ontogenetically* and *phylogenetically:* that is, both in terms of the evolution of the individual (Rom. 7:7–13) and in terms of the evolution of the human species (Gal. 3; Rom. 5:12–21). What is more, in both cases Paul wrestles constantly with logical questions in an immobilist perspective. That is why he would fall into flagrant contradictions unless he recognized the ambiguity of a process in which something good could progressively turn into something quite the opposite and vice versa.

    1. It would be interesting to begin by defining what Paul understands by *law,* but his writings offer us no such thing. What is more, any possible definition would destroy the evolutionary perspective just indicated.

So we would do well here to note how Paul describes his relationship—and that of humanity—with sin *before* the law. But we must remember that in Paul's view a transgression against an expressed mandate (which foreshadowed the future law) did exist at the beginning of time. As far as the individual is concerned, Paul sees the beginning of every individual's history as some sort of latent sin, even though he has not yet been confronted with the precepts of the law. That latent sin cannot be described in any greater detail.

How does Paul characterize this situation prior to the law? Paul considers early mankind, both the pagans and the line of patriarchs that founded Israel. He refers explicitly to the lapse of time "from Adam to Moses" (Rom. 5:14), excluding both ends as we shall see. The corresponding situation in the human individual is the age of infancy: "There was a time when, in the absence of law, I was fully alive; but when the commandment came . . . " (Rom. 7:9).[26]

What does Paul say about man's moral situation during this period? Firstly he says that a responsibility always exists in the case of human beings. Even at this primitive stage human existence is subject to a just judgment by God. Secondly he says that man possesses something with which to measure his conduct against God's judgment. However primitive he may be, however unaware of any commandment he may be, he possesses a "common sense" that tells him what he should or should not do. Thirdly Paul says that with this criterion human beings have grounds for defense and for accusation in their conduct, even though no fulfillment or transgression of commandments is involved. Note that they have grounds for defense as well as for indictment. Man has not only evil deeds but also good works, and the latter may be even better than the ones displayed by those who have explicit knowledge of the law later on (cf. Rom. 2:26–27).

Here is what Paul himself has to say: "When Gentiles who do not possess the law carry out its precepts by the light of nature,[27] then, although they have no law, they are their own law, for they display the effect of the law inscribed on their hearts.[28] Their conscience is called as witness, and their own thoughts argue the case on either side, against them or even for them, on the day when God judges the secrets of human hearts through Christ Jesus" (Rom. 2:14–16).

But we have as yet only touched the surface of what Paul sees at this human stage, and that brings us to our fourth point. In referring to sin, Paul seems to say two contradictory things. The first thing he says is that in this stage "sin was already in the world" to the point where "death held sway from Adam to Moses, even over those who had not sinned as Adam did" (Rom. 5:13–14). The sin of Adam occurred in the face of a commandment. But a commandment is not required for sin to be operative and to introduce the rule of death over human existence. The important point to note in this passage is that once moral conscience awakens in man and he allows himself to act against its dictates, then he is caught in the sway of death. This is not simply some external punishment. For that some sort of reckoning of sin would have to exist, but Paul says explicitly that "in the absence of law no reckoning is kept of sin" (Rom. 5:13)[29]

It seems clear that Paul's thinking is pointing to this: even in the absence of law, man destroys himself if he follows his desires without taking his conscience into account (cf. Rom. 1:24,26,28). Human existence can be maintained as such only by exerting a certain amount of violence against the instinctive, innate tendency to follow the easy way.

But that brings us to our fifth point. When no law from God exists to point out what this violence should be, what the basis of reaction against the instinctive is, then man is not confronted with another danger just as great as sin and death: i.e., the danger of *surrendering himself* to the law just as one might surrender himself to the instinctive. The fact is that exegesis has slipped up in the case of the term that Paul uses to characterize the period we are examining: "In the absence of law no reckoning is kept of sin" (Rom. 5:13). The term *reckoning* has been considered in terms of legal categories ("impute" in the sense of charging with an offense), when in Paul it has a markedly existential sense. It designates something that is "taken into account," that defines one's existence, as the more modern translation suggests. Thus it is something that constitutes a goal for the whole man.

How is someone defined as just? Who is "reckoned" to have a righteousness that "justifies" his existence? So long as man does not have the law to hold up as a mirror to his own life, the rationale of his existence *cannot be to avoid sin.* One who is struggling for his very existence is not even tempted to play it out in terms of culpability or nonculpability.

So that brings us to our sixth point. The vital attitude in question, the one that is not a surrender to one's own desires and mechanisms for the easy way out, constitutes a *faith*. It is essentially trust, and it does not really matter whether it gives a name to him who is truly its foundation. Hence in a religious world such as Paul's, pagans (i.e., those who do not know God) and Jews are embraced under one judgment. And that one judgment must necessarily be a response to one and the same existential attitude:

> What room then is left for human pride? It is excluded. And on what principle? The keeping of the law would not exclude it, but faith does. For our argument is that a man is justified by faith quite apart from success in keeping the law. Do you suppose God is the God of the Jews alone? Is he not the God of the Gentiles also? Certainly, of Gentiles also, if it be true that God is one. And he will therefore justify both the circumcised in virtue of their faith, and the uncircumcised through their faith (Rom. 3:27–30).

And this is not a new condition that becomes valid in history from the time of Christ, as is evident from the fact that Paul goes on to apply it to a period of humanity that is viewed as being prior to the law: the age of Abraham (cf. Rom. 4:1–11).

2. With this data in mind, perhaps we can begin to comprehend the apparent contradiction we just pointed out. On the one hand, prior to the law "sin was already in the world." On the other hand, "in the absence of law, sin is a dead thing" (Rom. 7:8). How can we reconcile these two statements? In what sense does the law give life to a sin that was already alive and kicking in the world?

In trying to resolve this contradiction in the relationship between law and sin, we will undoubtedly be able to spell out more clearly the nature of the law about which Paul is speaking.

From what we have already seen about the period "prior to the law," we know that Paul is talking about the law that appears on the Hebrew scene with Moses (cf. Rom. 4:13; Gal. 3:17–20).

Paul distinguishes between the law embodied in the very first part of Scripture and the law deriving from Moses, the latter being "the law" in the strict sense. But this distinction in itself does not clearly define the content of the word. We are often inclined to associate this word with the summary statement known as the Decalogue. But in fact the legislation attributed to Moses by Scripture takes in two additional planes: the sociopolitical organization of the Israelite nation and the organization of their religious life.

On several occasions Paul refers to concrete items of this "law" that steps on the human scene in and through the Israelite nation. And it is noteworthy that these items have to do with the three areas we have just mentioned. In one case Paul cites precepts of the Decalogue such as: "Thou shalt not covet" (Rom. 7:7; cf. Rom.2:21–22). In the second case Paul is talking about the fact that Christ liberates from the law, and he says something that is important for our considerations here. He attributes the deepest separations that exist between human beings, along with their consequent array of rights and duties, to the law: "Thus the law was a kind of tutor in charge of us until Christ. . . . And now . . . the tutor's charge is at an end. . . . There is no such thing as Jew and Greek, slave and freeman, male and female; for you are all one person in Christ Jesus" (Gal. 3:24–28; see also Eph. 2:15; 1 Cor. 12:13). In the third case, the law that Paul speaks about goes beyond the Decalogue and includes religious ordinances (e.g., circumcision) which do not belong to it (Gal. 5:2–6; Rom.2:25–29).

What are we to say about the value of a *law* which is understood in these terms? In reading Paul we must not forget that he is projecting the law that comes from Christ back over the period of the older law. In other words, he is talking about the law from the standpoint of our liberation from it.

It is not surprising, then, that his more personal judgments are unfavorable. Nor is it surprising that when he is faced with the outright question as to whether the law is evil, he does not go so far as to say it is. For he is viewing it in terms of the overall plan within which it was inserted. In other words, Paul's comments on the law would be contradictory if he were not viewing it in evolutionary terms. That is why his most clearcut passage on the value and worth of the law is formulated in terms of a comparison between the situation of a child and the situation of an adult vis-à-vis an external authority (cf. Gal. 4:1–7).

With this in mind we can cite two sets of passages that sum up Paul's view of the positive values and negative attributes embodied in the law. On the one hand the law provides man with guidelines: "instructed by the law, you know right from wrong" (Rom. 2:17–18; see also 7:10–12). On the other hand it has a negative side, as these passages bring out forcefully: "Law intruded into this process to multiply law-breaking" (Rom. 5:20); "Then what of the law? It was added to make wrongdoing a legal offence" (Gal. 3:19; see also Gal. 3:21–23; 1 Cor 9:56).[30]

Thus the law is relativized when it is viewed from the standpoint of its goal: Christ. It has a necessary function to play as a stage in human development, but it is not the embodiment of an absolute divine will. For this reason Paul takes pains to point out that the law "was promulgated through angels, and there was an intermediary; but an intermediary is not needed for one party acting alone, and God is one" (Gal.3:19–20).

The mediation points up a necessity deriving from man's side. And in line with Paul's thought it is this: man has to be guided by a more certain and definite authority in those areas where his survival and progress can no longer depend on his basic instincts. But as Paul sees it, man also pays a price for this new-found certainty of the law. Man's preoccupation with sin and his recognition that something is prohibited even though his instincts tend in that direction give one the definite impression that sin, which always existed, has taken on new life with the coming of the law:

What follows? Is the law identical with sin? Of course not. But except through law I should never have known what it was to covet, if the law had not said, "Thou shalt not covet." Through that commandment sin found its opportunity, and produced in me all kinds of wrong desires. In the absence of law, sin is a dead thing. There was a time when, in the absence of law, I was fully alive; but when the commandment came, sin sprang to life and I died. The commandment which should have led to life proved in my experience to lead to death, because sin found its opportunity in the commandment, seduced me, and through the commandment killed me (Rom. 7:7–11).

So there is a two-way dialectic in the law. When the law is turned into an absolute, it serves the purposes of sin. When the law splinters on the hard rock of history, it is turned into a relative thing and can then serve as the basis for a new, more mature, and more creative morality.

When Paul, or one of the disciples in his circle, writes to Timothy, he provides a succinct statement of the law's value if it is used aright: "We all know that the law is an excellent thing, *provided we treat it as law,* recognizing that it is not aimed at good citizens, but at the lawless and unruly" (1 Tim. 1:8–9; our italics). Here the author is referring to the inability of the instincts to know and therefore practice what is good in circumstances that are too complex for them to handle and solve.

On the other side of the coin, however, providing instinct with the help of an external thing like the law can set in motion something just as deadly as the original instinct. Paraphrasing Paul, we could call this something else a "super-instinct." It trusts wholly in the law and thus turns the law into a regressive outlook and attitude. The search for righteousness may then turn into something that is not the right use of the law but the direct opposite: "Gentiles, *who made no effort after righteousness,* nevertheless achieved it, a righteousness based on faith; whereas Israel *made great efforts after a law of righteousness,* but never attained to it. Why was this? Because their efforts were not based on faith, but (as they supposed) *on deeds*" (Rom. 9:30–32; our italics).

Because of the law, a whole society acquires an outlook and attitude that is the direct opposite of authentic progress: "Now law is not at all a matter of having faith. We read, 'he who does this shall gain life by what he does.' Christ bought us freedom from the curse of the law" (Gal. 3:12–13). Close attention should be paid to the fact that here the term *law* no longer designates a code of laws. Instead it designates an attitude that attributes absolute and decisive efficacy to its carrying out. So it is not surprising that the law paradoxically produces a backlash, engendering the same bondage as sin does: "Scripture has declared the whole world to be prisoners in subjection to sin, so that faith in Jesus Christ may be the ground on which the promised blessing is given . . . Before this faith came, we were close prisoners in the custody of law" (Gal. 3:22–23).

The fertile ambiguity of the term *law* in Paul's writings shows us that sin and evolution are intimately bound up with each other in many recurrent ways. Only an evolutionary outlook can account for Paul's conception of sin. And in turn only the decisive force of sin permits an evolutionary outlook to remain dialectical and progressively evolutionary.

With respect to the latter, one might well ask whether Paul's conception of the law does not see the cycle ended and our definitive liberation already achieved. Consider this passage: "For sin shall no longer be your master, because you are no longer under law, but under the grace of God" (Rom. 6:14). Or this passage: "In Christ Jesus the life-giving law of the Spirit [i.e., grace] has set you free from the law of sin and death" (Rom. 8:2). The end of the law, in the twofold sense of *telos* (completion and culmination), is Christ (cf. Rom. 10:4; Gal. 3:23–24).

What then are the individual and social possibilities of man under the new "law of the Spirit," under the grace or "liberty" of Christ—these being synonymous terms in Paul's language? The exegetes have different opinions on this question.[31] But Paul does talk about an inner division in man (cf. Rom. 7:14–23). In his inmost heart man recognizes the "spiritual" law[32] but his fulfillment of it continues to obey statistical laws that sheer away from true liberty. On the basis of what he says in this connection it is our feeling that Paul is pointing to an indefinite prolongation of the law dialectic even after Christ's liberation. Here, as in the case of John's notion of "the world," victory is a certainty in principle. But it is being realized in a cyclical manner, in which sin plays its decisive and ambiguous role at every turn.

This characteristic manner makes manifest the equivocalness of any norm in an evolutionary perspective. A univocal valuation of law is not only un-Christian but clearly immobilist.

NOTES

1. Sigmund Freud, *Civilization and Its Discontents*, Eng. trans. by James Strachey (New York: W. W. Norton, 1962), pp. 64–66.

2. "If the self-preservative instincts are also of a libidinous kind, then perhaps we have no other instincts at all than libidinous ones. There are at least no other apparent" (Freud, *Beyond the Pleasure Principle*, Eng. trans. by C. J. M. Hubbock, GBWW 54:658).

3. "Our standpoint was a dualistic one from the beginning, and is so today more sharply than before, since we no longer call the contrasting tendencies *egoistic* and *sexual* instincts, but *life-instincts* and *death-instincts*" (*ibid.*, pp. 658–659).

4. See Herbert Marcuse, *Eros and Civilization*, (New York: Vintage Books Edition, 1962), pp. 21–22.

5. Freud, " 'Civilized' Sexual Morality and Modern Nervousness," in *Collected Papers*, Eng. trans. by Joan Riviere (London: Hogarth Press and the Institute of Psychoanalysis, 1948), II, 82.

6. They really correspond to the successive stages of Freud's thinking. But in the last stage they are intermingled, which points to the indecisiveness of Freud's final thought.

7. "After sublimation, the erotic component no longer has the power to bind the whole of the destructive elements that were previously combined with it, and these are released in the form of inclinations to aggression and destruction" (Freud, *The Ego and the Id*, Eng. trans. by Joan Riviere, GBWW 54:715).

8. Freud, *A General Introduction to Psycho-Analysis*, Eng. trans. by Joan Riviere (GBWW 54:592).

9. Freud, *New Introductory Lectures on Psycho-Analysis*, Eng. trans. by W. J. H. Sprott, GBWW 54:838.

10. Freud, *Civilization and Its Discontents*, *op. cit.*, p. 51.

11. Freud, *New Introductory Lectures on Psycho-Analysis*, *op. cit.*, p. 838.

12. Freud, *Civilization and Its Discontents*, *op. cit.*, pp. 55–56. Indeed "no other technique for the conduct of life attaches the individual so firmly to reality as laying emphasis on work.... The possibility it offers of displacing a large amount of libidinal components, whether narcissistic, aggressive or even erotic, on to professional work and on to the human relations connected with it lends it a value by no means second to what it enjoys as something indispensible to the preservation and justification of existence in society" (*ibid.*, footnote 1, p. 27).

13. *Ibid.*, pp. 55–56.

14. *Ibid.*, p. 68. But then Freud goes on to say: "But *man's natural aggressive instinct* . . . opposes the programme of civilization. This aggressive instinct is *the derivative and the main representative of the death instinct*" (*ibid.*, our italics). The ambivalence of the term *death instinct* in Freud's use of language presents a serious problem. What sort of death is he talking about? If we consider the most radical passages of Freud on the totality of the instinctive world, he is talking about a rejection of any and all pain, a regression to the calmness of our mother's womb. If that is the correct interpretation, then death and aggression are simply an end result, not a goal sought for its own sake. How then is this "aggression" by passivity to be translated into "domination of nature," work, and the destruction of external objects? It is not clear whether Freud moves unjustifiably from death as result to death as an intention, or whether he does not also see aggressiveness as dominated by culture as regression to a new and satisfying maternal womb. Social adaptation would be regression of this sort, in other words. That is Marcuse's opinion (*Eros and Civilization*, *op. cit.*, Chapter 5).

15. According to Marcuse, this indecision "keeps Freud's late metapsychology in that state of suspense and depth which makes it one of the great intellectual ventures in the science of man" (*Eros and Civilization*, Chapter 2, *op. cit.*, p. 26).

16. *Ibid.*, Chapter 10, p. 192.

17. In the CLARIFICATION of Chapter I we have examined several passages where Freud seems to oppose the demands of Agape in the name of Eros. See, for example, *Civilization and Its Discontents*, *op. cit.*, pp. 55–57.

18. Later on in this volume we shall try to tackle another important question left aside here: Can a culture impose excessive and unnecessary repression on people?

19. In a letter of March 30, 1954,Teilhard de Chardin makes this simple statement: "Like you, I certainly think that the solution to the problem of Eros and Agape simply lies in evolution." Cited by Madeleine Barthélémy-Madaule, *Bergson et Teilhard de Chardin* (Paris: Ed. du Seuil, 1963), p. 49, n. 1.

20. Piet Schoonenberg, *Man and Sin: A Theological View,* Eng. trans. by Joseph Donceel (Notre Dame: University of Notre Dame Press, 1965), p. 4.

21. *Ibid.*, p. 23.

22. This topic will be the object of a forthcoming work by this author. But Chapter V of this volume, along with its CLARIFICATIONS, and the Conclusions offer starting points for further work on the subject.

23. See Chapter IV, CLARIFICATION IV. Up to now we have no example of the State disappearing completely. Such an event would probably be the sign of a phenomenon which we might describe as follows: the minorities change and become majorities, or else the latter acquire qualities proper to the former and become active subjects of history.

24. Later on we shall see that as evolution gradually passes into the hands of humanity itself, the mass element does not remain a static datum. The minorities cannot progress without raising the mass that is the basis of their operation. This will be the realistic challenge to human sin.

25. "At this stage one may ask what gains accrue to the two individuals from this development. The most important gain is that each will be able to predict the other's actions. Concomitantly, the interaction of both becomes predictable. The 'There he goes again' becomes a 'There *we* go again.' This relieves both individuals of a considerable amount of tension. They save time and effort, not only in whatever external tasks they might be engaged in separately or jointly, but in terms of their respective psychological economies. Their life together is now defined by a widening sphere of taken-for-granted routines. Many actions are possible on a low level of attention. . . . The construction of this background of routine in turn makes possible a division of labor between them, opening the way for innovations, which demand a higher level of attention" (Peter L. Berger and Thomas Luckmann, *The Social Construction of Reality,* New York: Doubleday Anchor Books, 1967, p. 57).

26. This is the most prevailing, and we would say the most logical, interpretation of this passage. Stanislas Lyonnet (Spanish trans. *La Historia de la Salvación en la Carta a los Romanos,* Salamanca: Ed. Sígueme, 1967; original not ascertained) defends another interpretation. According to him, this interval is the time Adam lived in paradise before his sin. Aside from the fact that his arguments are weak, even his interpretation would serve our proposals here.

27. That is, "are guided by conscience," as the Jerusalem Bible comments in a note (New York: Doubleday, 1966), note c on Rom. 2:14.

28. In biblical literature the *heart* is not so much the seat of man's affective life as it is the seat of thought, judgment, and understanding.

29. Even under the rule of the law death is not just an external punishment. This is proven by what Paul adds in the very passage where he talks in the first person about the condition of the child without law: "When the commandment came, sin sprang to life and I died. . . . Sin became more sinful than ever" (Rom. 7:9–10,13).

30. Some people still claim that Paul never arrived at a coherent solution to the problem of how to value the law. They claim this because they do not accept the radical thoroughness with which Paul speaks about man's liberation from the

law. Remaining within an Old Testament outlook, they will only recognize an "interiorization" of the law, not its replacement by a creative love (see Volume I, Chapter V).

31. As we see it, the division depends more on an overall conception of the relationship between Jesus and the end of time than on the concrete interpretation of Romans 7. See Volume II, Chapter III, CLARIFICATION III.

32. The force of our argument does not reside primarily in Paul's use of the first person and the present tense. It resides in his use of the term "spiritual law." As we have seen, he uses this strictly to designate Christ's "life-giving law of the Spirit" and not for the law of Moses.

CHAPTER THREE

Guilt at the Acme of Evolution

In the previous chapter we established what we feel to be one bridgehead between the evolutionary conception of the universe and the Christian theology of sin. What is more, in the closing paragraphs of the main article we alluded to an idea that may provide us with a key for establishing our other bridgehead. In this case we shall start from the other end, from divine revelation, and try to find something that is better understood in evolutionary terms.

In the last chapter we saw that when one and the same reality (e.g., Christ) has to be pictured at two different points in time, this signifies something that can be expressed more properly within an evolutionary perspective. When the past and the present—or the present and the future—are juxtaposed and presented as being simultaneous, this is our usual and most satisfactory way of representing a gradual transformation. For example, that is what we would do if we had to explain our chronological experience of childhood, adolescense, and adulthood to some being who had no personal experience of time and change. In all sincerity and seriousness we would tell such a being that we are the same person we were earlier and that we are not the same person we were. Only the seemingly contradictory affirmation of both statements can convey the idea of an evolution to the mind. And this applies to the evolution of the world and our own personal evolution.

With this key conception in mind, then, let us explore New Testament revelation to find themes which are connected with sin and redemption and which seem to call for a "structural," evolutionary outlook.

Section I

Even though his Gospel appears only a few decades after the three Synoptic Gospels, we are surprised by the universal perspective—"cosmic" perspective would be more exact etymologically—that John attributes to the teaching of Jesus.

According to the Synoptic Gospels, Jesus provokes a conflict against the hypocritical and hardhearted religion that was then official in Israel. In John's Gospel, however, Jesus is fighting against a force that has taken on other dimensions. This force is not labelled "sin," [1] a term that appears only thirty-five times in John's writings. It is designated by the simple Greek word that describes the structure of the universe: *cosmos* (i.e., the world). This term is used almost three times as often as the word *sin*, one hundred times to be exact, and in fifty-one cases it clearly seems to have a pejorative sense. [2]

Thus the later conception of Christianity as a message dealing with individual morality and personal redemption must strike us as a serious distortion. The sin that the Son of God comes to overcome and take away is "*the* sin *of the world*" (John: 29, our italics; note the singular). This single, universal sin is not a free act, it is a state of enslavement: "Everyone who commits sin is a *slave*" (John 8:34 our italics; "sin" again is singular). This sin cannot be reduced to a particular act of infringing the law, which would not bring enslavement; and what liberates man from it is knowing the truth (John 8:32). Thus the sin of the world is the structure by virtue of which man's actions are obscure to man himself insofar as their real import is concerned. Without fear of making a mistake, we could say that the alienating sin of the world is "ideology."

The fact is that the truth that brings freedom is not a matter of theory but a matter of praxis. This is proven by the fact that only the honest man comes to Christ, the light, so that it may be clearly seen "that God is in all he does" (John 3:21). The honest man "does truth." By contrast, bad men hate the light of Christ and avoid it, "for fear their practices should be shown up" (John 3:20).

But what exactly is this "world" that is opposed to Christ? To answer this question let us first look at the Prologue of John's Gospel: The Word "was in the *world*; but the *world*, though it owed its being to him, did not recognize him. He entered his own realm, and his own would not receive him. But to all who did receive him . . . " (John 1:10–12). In the first instance we could say that the "world" simply designates a place or locale. In the second instance it has more complex connotations; it designates mankind, which should accept the Word because it owes its existence to him. It is a world "under obligation." But this "world" has already taken on a negative character; it signifies mankind, but this text notes that human beings have not accepted their obligation to the Word. The verse indicates a collective rejection, at least in quantitative terms.

We get a clearer picture of this rejection in the two following verses.

The rejection has not been total. There were some who were "his own" and had recognized him. In this case the reference is undoubtedly to Israel, the People of Yahweh. And the process is repeated. The Word takes another step and comes to his own. His own do not accept him; once again there is a collective rejection. And once again there are some who do receive and accept him.

What does all this mean? Insofar as the use of the term *world* is concerned, the meaning seems clear enough. The rejection was so overwhelming in quantitative terms that it is applied to the "world" as a whole when in fact it really applies to the vast majority. In the case of "his own" too, the rejection is of equivalent proportions and evokes the same expression. Even though some did receive him, "his own" as a whole rejected him. The proportion is such in quantitative terms that it is justifiable to say that "the world" and "his own" rejected the Word. Semantically speaking, the exceptions do not count.

At this point our question is whether we are dealing simply with a statistical fact or with something structural as well. The very choice of the term *world* (*cosmos*) seems to indicate the latter. So does the rest of John's Gospel, since it applies the term to those who are opposed to Jesus rather than to the multitude of non-Jews.

To answer this question we must recapture a feeling of surprise that has been dulled by familiarity with the Gospel text. It should surprise us to find that Jesus attacks his adversaries for a rather curious reason: they "belong to this world" or are "of the world." As if they could *not belong* to this world! As if he and his disciples were not of this world (cf. John 8:23; 17:14,15,19)!

What, then, does "the world" signify in Jesus' use of the term? In trying to answer this question, the first element we come across is the notion of impotence and inability: "The world *cannot* hate you" (John 7:7); "Where I am going you *cannot* come. . . . You belong to this world below" (John 8:22–23); "The world *cannot* receive" the Spirit of truth (John 14:17).

With this key notion in our grasp, many other passages referring to the "world" unlock their meaning to us. Christ's rejection by the world, which was mentioned in the Prologue to the Gospel, is not simply a statistical result; it is a constant. Radically incapable of recognizing Christ, the world as such (i.e., as a structure) is not an object of Jesus' prayer: "I am not praying for the world" (John 17:9). Its intrinsic mechanism does not pay heed to the truth and its ambassadors. It has no respect for solid reasons: "If the world hates you, it hated me first, as you know well. If you belonged to the world, the world would love its own. . . . A servant is not greater than his master. . . . He who hates me, hates my Father. . . . This text in their Law had to come true: 'They hated me without reason' " (John 15:18–25).

That is why Jesus is quite sure of himself in attributing to the world attitudes and motivations that remain constant and that would be inexplicable if they were applied to a free individual: "the world neither sees nor knows him" (John 14:17); "the world will see me no longer, but you will" (John 14:19); "peace such as the world cannot give" (John 14:27); "because you do not belong to the world . . . the world hates you" (John 15:19); "the world hates them because they are strangers in the world" (John 17:14); "the reason why the godless world does not recognize us is that it has not known him [Christ]" (1 John 3:1); false prophets "are of that world, and so therefore is their teaching; that is why the world listens to them" (1 John 4:5); the whole godless world lies in the power of the evil one" (1 John 5:19). These attitudes should not cause us wonder. They are the very fabric and nature of "the world" (1 John 3:1).

This brings us to a second question. Whence comes this structural incapacity, this determinism which makes the world a fixed and finished totality that is as predictable as a machine in Christ's eyes?

It derives from the fact that we are dealing here with a social mechanism that is essentially conservative. The functions that go to make up the world are caught in a vicious circle that opposes all novelty. A key passage sums up this circularity: "They are of that world, and so therefore is their teaching; that is why the world listens to them" (1 John 4:5). This vicious circle of closed-circuit communication is "the spirit of error" (1 John 4:6); it is a radical incapacity to receive "the Spirit of truth" (John 14:17).

In other words, conservative ideology deceives by establishing a closed circuit in which everything is fixed and decided—whether it be love, or desire, or knowledge. "If you belonged to the world, the world would love its *own*; but because you do not belong to the world . . . for that reason the world hates you" (John 15:19). That is to say: Don't be surprised by this hatred because the world only loves what it has already decided to love and hates everything which lies outside and which it has already decided to hate from the start (cf. John 17:14).

In like manner the world shows up as a system of desires that are satisfied within it. Again it is a closed circle (cf. 1 John 2:15).

In praxis the lure of the easy way plays its ideological role by lending support to the social syntheses that have already been worked out; they are the simplest because they are already in use. The easy way does not recognize evolution. The opportune moment in history can only be grasped by those who get beyond the conservative and mechanical bonds of the easy way out. It is they who possess the "Spirit of truth," for truth is not a theoretical thing but a light shed on what we do (cf. John 3:19–21).

This feature of the world, its a-historicity, is clearly brought out when the relatives of Jesus approach him with a very logical request. If he is doing wondrous things, then he should do them openly out in the world because they are part of its system of supply and demand: "If you really are doing such things as these, show yourself to the world" (John 7:4).[3] To be sure, Jesus is going to show himself to the world. But he is not going to do it by submitting to its mechanism. Instead he is going to cast his light on it and thereby dispel the lie that paralyzes it. Its conservative ideology will be judged by the patent power of his truth. But that entails something else, as we shall see later: namely, waiting for the right moment. The world is not a monolith. There are critical moments that are open to the truth. So Jesus is waiting for his "hour," his "moment of opportunity."

This is what underlies his response to his relatives. They would have him become a well-adjusted cog in the world's gear mechanism. His response stresses the importance of the "right moment": "The right time for me has not yet come, but any time is right for you. The world cannot hate you; but it hates me for exposing the wickedness of its ways" (John 7:6–7). There is no real opportunity, no right moment, in a closed conservative system. Real opportunity must come from a sudden glimpse of an ongoing process beyond the trammels of mechanical repetition and the enclosed moment. Only then does the moment become fraught with meaning, efficacy, and truth; only then does it become the right moment.

To acquire this historical perspective we must break through the self-evident and accustomed aura that surrounds everything within a closed, self-sufficient mechanism. We must realize, for example, that what seems normal to us today is the result of some novelty in a past day: that its newness has been stripped away by dint of habit and custom.

In one of the harshest scenes in John's Gospel (8:12 ff.), Jesus encounters "the world" with its worst features. It is the world turned into a lie, a frozen mental outlook incapable of deeper comprehension. The Pharisees will not accept the truth about Jesus. He is what he says he is. They reject his teaching, confident that mere descent from Abraham is enough to preserve them from danger and error. But in reality it is not Abraham that is influencing them, it is the devil and his lie. They are enslaved to a devilish lie, which now alienates them from the truth and makes them carry out the devil's wishes as their own (cf. John 8:44). Once this devilish lie has turned into a social mechanism, it brings death to man. Conservative ideology is homicidal *"from the beginning"* (John

8:44; our italics); it destroys man and his vocation in history. This was true from the beginning of time, even as it is true from the time when the light first started to combat it.

To overcome this obstacle is, as it were, to be born over again (John 3:5–7); for it entails giving up security and certainty and accepting the "crisis"—i.e., the judgment—provoked when the light is focused on the true import of man's praxis.

Thus the fundamental sin under consideration here is not man's individual infraction of the law but his political negation of history.

Section II

This brings us to a third decisive element in our characterization of "the world," one that is intimately bound up with our remarks about entropy in the preceding chapter.

So far we have tried to explain why Jesus constantly uses the term *world* to refer to the force that is opposed to his own work. But we cannot overlook the other side of the coin. To a lesser extent, which is quite considerable for all that, the "world" shows up as the obligatory locale, the indispensable precondition, and even the terminus for the salvation and love brought by the Word. To put it briefly: "God loved the world so much that he gave his only Son. . . . It was not to judge the world that God sent his Son into the world, but that through him the world might be saved" (John 3:16–17; cf. John 12:47). Jesus is recognized as the "Saviour of the world" (John 4:42 and 1 John 4:14) because he takes away its sin (John 1:29) and gives it life (John 6:33,51). And while it is certain that Jesus' disciples, like Jesus himself, are not "of the world," it is also certain that Christ's redemption is extended not only to his own but to "the sins of all the world" (1 John 2:2).

Thus one of the most recurrent themes in John's writings is the positive, love-filled, salvific character of the Son of God's entry into the world.[4] While it is certain that the world is ruled by a force that is called the "prince of lies," it ever remains the community of mankind. It continues to be the one and only human reality, the recompense for all our efforts, suffering, and even death. Christ's disciples are taken or chosen *from the world*, but in order that they may enter it and remain there (cf. John 17:6,15,18).

The world cannot be conquered from outside. What is more, Jesus does not seek to conquer it for his own sake but in order to liberate mankind, which is oppressed by its destructive lie. Here again we see the same point that was brought up in our earlier discussion of entropy: the frail and inert syntheses of a simpler sort are a precondition for the victory of higher quality. And the qualitative victory here is the *light* of truth shed on the ideological mechanisms that tend to conserve man's social structure.

On the other hand a certain "dose" of this mechanical, monolithic, conservative solidarity vis-à-vis disruptive novelty is necessary. It is the indispensable basis for the existence of a society, a world. It must exist so that the new message of liberation will not resound in a vacuum of isolated individual subjects. Only when it is present can one talk about coming "to bear witness to the truth" (John 18:37).

Insofar as the moment of crisis itself is concerned. Jesus ushers it in to the extent that the "gratuitousness" of the world's hatred becomes clear. Its hatred of him is without good reason. Society cannot really justify the defenses its puts up against a life-giving message. And this message will show up the lie that posed as truth and rejected real truth (cf. John 9:39). The revelation of Jesus' love, which is totally devoid of egotism, is simultaneously his glory, the salvation of the world, judgment on the world, and the overthrow of the one that has dominated it up to now (cf. John 13: 15:22; 12:31; 16:11).

But here we come upon a point that is most important in trying to establish a link between revelation and evolution: the world is conquered and *at the same time* not conquered. For Jesus, as we have already seen, saving the world means introducing his light into it. His judgment is not that of some outside judge pronouncing sentence on a defendant with whom he is not involved. Jesus judges by the simple fact that he shares the life of the world and involves himself in it in truth.

How does Jesus describe the outcome of this judgment, which to some extent reproduces the judgment introduced by the ancient prophets? Note what he says: "Here lies the test. The light has come into *the world but men* preferred darkness to light because their deeds were evil" (John 3:19; our italics). The introduction of the light does not result in any mass conversion from evil to goodness. It is a victory *sui generis*. Jesus tells his disciples: "In the world you will have trouble. but courage! The victory is mine; I have conquered the world" (John 16:33). Even as he tells them of his victory, he reminds them that the opposing quantitative forces will continue to exist in the same disproportionate way. We would have pictured the victory of salvation in a different way. We would have imagined that the easy way would now be placed in the service of the law. But that is certainly not the way Jesus sees it (cf. John 15:18–20).

At another point Jesus remarks: "If I had not come and spoken to them, *they would not be guilty of sin*; but now *they have no excuse for their sin*"

(John 15:22; our italics). This is a key point. We know that Jesus does not provoke a *new* sin; he sheds light on what man is doing. But what man was doing mechanically was not sin, strictly speaking, even though it may have been wrong. Once Jesus has come with his message and witness, however, this line of action is shown to be sinful and the person who continues doing it has no excuse.

To put it another way: ideology, the recourse to the easy way out that precludes richer human syntheses, is not sin to the extent that it operates covertly. The conservative does not manipulate ideology, he believes in it. It is masked from his view. But once this mask is torn away, ideology is subject to judgment. Man must see his past and his present as a sin against human beings, because it is rooted in a devilish lie: "Your father is the devil and you choose to carry out your father's desires. He was a murderer from the beginning, and is not rooted in the truth" (John 8:44).

So once again we meet something that was expressed in an immobilist form but is best translated in evolutionary terms. Ideology is sin and is not sin because a gradual transformation is involved.

In qualitative terms every new and richer synthesis is due to a critical judgment fashioned in the minds of a few. Through them the new synthesis finds the mechanisms required for its preservation. Facility, the easy way out, helps it along by conserving it. At the same time facility also closes it to. more difficult and even richer syntheses. The latter would have been fatal at the time the previous synthesis was established, because no minority can transform all reality on its own. But once the mechanisms have become an interlocking support, danger begins to show up from the other side. What was a minority creation becomes a mass reality; a new synthesis requires a new "right moment." It must wait for the "hour" of a new minority who will show people that what was once new light has now become sin.

Section III

What we have said so far indicates that in the sin opposed to Jesus John saw something besides its social and conservative aspects. These features had already been descried in the Synoptic Gospels.[5] Operating through immobilist mental conceptions, John perceived that Christ's redemption was operating in an *evolutionary* framework. The dialectic of negative versus positive, defeat versus victory, and quantity versus quality dovetails point by point with the notion of entropy which holds true for the evolution of the whole universe.

Now one might be inclined to say that there is nothing very original in this notion of a dialectic between habit and conservatism on the one hand and innovation and crisis on the other hand. That may be true, but we would still maintain that it was an original notion in a culture whose most deep-rooted outlook (Stoicism) pictured nature dictating both the physical and the social order from all eternity and for all eternity. We would also say that it was an original idea in the contemporary religious world, where both the Hebrew religion and the mystery religions looked for quick, definitive salvation in one way or another. And even if it was not an original notion, it certainly served as a powerful corrective against messianic doctrines in which both the preservation of existing society and its rapid transformation seemed immune to critical questioning at key moments. Such critical questioning must be a permanent factor, and it must have adequate room to find expression as such.[6]

This evolutionary outlook is not the "content" of the Christian message, however, and we are not interested in dwelling on its originality. What we have tried to show in this chapter is that such an outlook is *the key* to Christianity. In other words the whole Christian message—and particularly the relationship between sin and redemption—should be viewed from that angle of vision.

All the elements fall into place within this perspective. From the very beginning the whole universe is molded by a thrust toward liberation grounded on truth in praxis. From the very beginning the universe also shows a proclivity toward facile, conservative solutions. As time goes on, these degraded syntheses must defend themselves more and more fiercely against the critical light that points the way toward more difficult but richer syntheses.

This profound duality is not to be identified with any specific human group. It is bound up with a deep, underlying tendency that dominates majorities on any and every plane. The triumph of quality is ensured by the liberative power of the Word who is Light. His power traverses the whole pageant of evolution, but the quantitative ratio between majorities and minorities, sin and grace, the easy way to facile syntheses and the hard way to richer syntheses, remains the same.

The progressive course of liberative salvation is inextricably bound up with the Word in this situation. It does not take what is intrinsically difficult and make it easy. But at each moment of "crisis" the Word, who launched the whole universe toward liberation from the very start, gives human beings and things the power to break up earlier worlds that have turned into mechanisms of mere repetitiveness and death.

This victory will always be the same. A quantitative death is followed by a qualitative victory. Then the latter is taken over by the very segment that continues to bow to the mechanisms of the world and to lean toward facile and inferior syntheses in individual and social life. "And I shall draw all men to myself, when I am lifted up from the earth" (John 12:32).[7]

NOTES TO CHAPTER THREE

1. Our word *sin* has an individual connotation that does not fit in well with the Greek term. The latter has a more structural connotation. Note the difference between *hamartía* and *parábasis* in Paul's usage (CLARIFICATION IV in this chapter).

2. In eighty cases out of these hundred, the term cannot be interpreted neutrally as a place where events take place without having any instrinsic relationship to each other.

3. Judas formulates the same demand in a question: "Lord, what can have happened, that you mean to disclose yourself to us alone and not to the world?" (John 14:22).

4. See the following passages, for example: John 10:36; 12:46; 16:28; 17:18; 18:37; 1 John 4:9.

5. See our treatment of the demonic in CLARIFICATION IV of this chapter.

6. "Democracy" and "socialism" are systematically expressed in immobilist terms despite the fact that both have resulted from critical revolutions and had an evolutionary conception at their origins.

7. Not "all things" (neuter gender), as the Latin version has it. The same fate awaits Christ's disciples. See John 16:2 in addition to the texts already cited.

CLARIFICATIONS

I. ORIGINAL SIN IN CATECHESIS AND POLITICAL CONSERVATISM

It may well be that we underestimate the impact of Christian catechesis about original sin on our individual and collective life.

1. Right away the image of an original fall that breaks up God's plan vitiates any and every attempt to attribute total and thoroughgoing value to the historical process. After original sin man lives a fallen, "decadent" existence—a subhistory.

2. *Paradise* (a utopian future) is located in the past before the fall. By this very fact it cannot be the object of action in history. And *paradise* is also the name that traditional catechesis reserves for that which lies beyond history: "heaven." History loses its intrinsic value content; it is turned into a *test* of each individual's existence.

3. The image of redemption, which in theory is victorious over original sin, is not an image-connoting power. The reason is very simple. It is not such an image because it does not call up the image of a victory. On the one hand there is nothing that restricts or conditions the spread of sin, whereas redemption appears to be nothing more than something offered; the latter is efficacious on the condition that man resorts to it through faith and baptism.[1] On the other hand this restrictive condition on the numerical, quantitative side is matched by an even more important one on the qualitative side. Even when sin is suppressed, its attraction remains intact and preponderant; we are still left to face concupiscence. Redemption seems to be a victory without any tangible consequences. In terms of the image it conjures up, it remains far inferior to original sin.

4. Original sin, prolonged by the victorious tendency to sin, must be resisted but never will be resisted enough. The idea of original sin calls up a spontaneous flood of images: the habits acquired from a "good" education, social legislation with its coercive measures, various restraints designed to reduce the effects of original sin.

5. In the "religious" imagination this gives rise to a repugnance toward any and every instinctive outlook, any deviation from the law, any

oposition to "good" habits and customs. In short, it fosters a repugnance toward anything and everything that threatens the established order. Everything that is violent, brutal, and instinctive is discredited as something deriving from sin, which refuses to accept the restraints of education and the legislation already in force.

6. As a result our traditional catechesis on sin, prescinding from the logical concatenation here, operates in only one sense insofar as class struggle is concerned. It becomes a natural ally and component of the mentality of the dominant class, justifying every unfavorable judgment passed on the violent and illegal vindications to which exploited people are often reduced in order to affirm their rights and their dignity.

It would be difficult to blame *theoretical* theology for directly inspiring this concatenation of images. But we can say that it has been insensitive to the impact it has had. It has given rise to a host of logically interconnected images, which in turn are translated into attitudes and value judgments. And the political content of these attitudes and value judgments give rise to the suspicion that its insensitivity is not accidental. While we would say that it is not a valid criticism of authentic Christianity, we feel that there is much to justify this observation of Marx: "These principles of Christianity explain all the vile actions to which the oppressed are subjected by their oppressors either as just chastisement for original sin . . . or as tests imposed on the elect by God in his wisdom." [2]

As we have noted, these two explanations are not in opposition but rather mutually interdependent. Paradoxically enough, their common coefficient is that they drain all transcendence out of history, wherein the destiny of the oppressed is played out. And we say "paradoxically" because Paul VI accuses Marxist ideology of this very thing. In one of his recent apostolic letters he indicates why the Christian cannot support Marxist doctrines. One of the reasons is that Marxism denies "any transcendent excellence to man, his personal history, or the history of the world." [3]

Here we are clearly dealing with a conflict in language. And the Christian has no right to evade this conflict by simply saying that history is important for Marxism but it does not have a transcendent Being at its acme in the Marxist view. This hasty insertion evades a critical question. We must examine the usual form in which the relationship between this transcendent Being and history is presented in Christian catechesis. We must see whether history is deprived of *transcendence* in this view as well, insofar as it is reduced to a *test* of the individual before God's judgment seat—as Marx claimed.

Even after Marx voiced this judgment, the so-called "social doctrine" of the Church continued to refer to original sin, to the irremediable loss of paradise in history, and to history as a testing ground for man. This proves quite clearly that the images we have been talking about have not had an impact solely on childish or superficial minds.

In 1939 Pius XII wrote an encyclical to the bishops of the United States. In it he says: "We are going to touch upon . . . the social question which . . . sows the seed of hatred and conflict between the *social classes.*" In the course of his remarks, he points to a fact and offers a justification for it: "The lesson that comes down to us from time immemorial is that there have always been rich people and poor people . . . God . . . has determined that there should be rich people and poor people in the world *so that virtues may be exercised and merits proven.*" [4]

Back in 1914 Benedict XV wrote this: "The effective practice of brotherly love does not consist in bringing about the disappearance of differences in class and living conditions . . . It consists in the fact that those at the top in some way stoop down to those below them and treat them not only justly . . . but also with kindness, gentleness, and patience." [5]

We can rightly ask why, in both case, it is taken for granted that any effort in history to avoid a class-ridden society is utopian. After discussing God's plan to test man in the text cited earlier, Pius XII alludes to "the inflexible condition of things." In Christian language this "reality" or "natural state of affairs" is almost always impreganted with the image of an initial fall whose consequences perdure.

In *Rerum novarum,* Leo XIII devotes a section to human inequality and notes that socialists are eagerly working to abolish it: "But this eager effort is futile and runs counter to the very nature of things." What exactly is "the very nature of things?" It is the situation that results from original sin and perdures: "Because the ills that followed upon sin are hard to bear . . . and of necessity must accompany man to the end of his life . . . no matter what efforts and concrete attempts man may make." [6]

In the light of these passages, it seems difficult to deny the justifiableness of Marx's observation about the real-life impact of a theology that is in theory orthodox. If in this volume we manage to show that original sin can be integrated into an evolutionary and dialectic presentation of God's liberative plan for human history, there will still remain the task of attacking the immobilist images of this sin that generate a conservative sociopolitical line of thought.

Here again we find the same thing that we found in CLARIFICATION I of the previous chapter: original sin, pictured in an immobilist framework rather than in an evolutionary one, ends up in *individualism.*

II. HORIZONTAL EVOLUTION VERSUS A VERTICAL GOD

The notion of "the immutable nature of things" was not the most decisive factor operating in the West. Even more decisive was a spirituality that was much more attuned to the people but equally antihistorical. For it operated on the assumption that the supernatural realm is *vertical* while the natural realm under historical control is *horizontal.*

The attitude of regarding the unpredictable as a *vertical* breakthrough by God is much more deeply rooted in Christian spirituality than we might think. Everything that takes the legs out from under man's prudential planning is viewed in this light. The maxim, "God writes straight with crooked lines," refers precisely to this sort of unexpected happening. God drops some good thing in our laps, as it were, when all indications point to things going the opposite way.

Even more than is the case with other virtues, the virtues of "prudence" and "wisdom" are qualified by the adjective "human" in a denigratory sense. In other words, they are equated with the horizontal, natural course of things.

This conception assumes that the supernatural is ushered in by great and wondrous happenings, not by any foreseeable evolution of things even if it be dialectical in nature. We will have occasion to see the element of truth contained in this conception when we discuss the inadequacies of any view that regards evolution as merely an accumulative, a-critical, straight-line process. We shall see that such a view does not represent the "nature of things," that it is an antinatural reduction of man and life to the more surface laws of inorganic matter.

It is not because it is horizontal that evolution may deny the supernatural. It does so if and when it is a dehumanizing thing. But at several points in this series we have pointed out that any attempt to equate vertical versus horizontal with grace versus nature is radically at variance with the kernel of the Christian message and its essential points.[7]

Here, however, it might prove more interesting to see this brand of spirituality in action—and in the recent past. In the years that followed World War II, a brand of theology known as "progressivism" produced a crisis. And even though the phenomenon was mainly confined to European Christianity, and to France in particular, it has real points of interest for Latin America.

Progressivism had its origin in the common struggle waged by Christians and Marxists within the French resistance movement. It was continued after the war in the struggle on behalf of the proletariat. In this struggle many Christians took part. Lay people and priests were involved, but the participation of the latter was greater in importance and public impact. The whole drama of the "worker priests" is framed within this context.

In order to appreciate this period and its successes and failures, we must recognize the fact that both sides in the Chruch—the "progressive" wing and those opposed to it—were part of a preconciliar Church. It is not just that people did not yet accept certain theoretical principles on which the"progressivist" outlook was based. The fact is that these principles had not yet been worked up satisfactorily. The more extreme expressions of the progressive tendency betray this lack, often ending up in simplistic viewpoints: e.g., acceptance of class struggle as the one and only motive force behind history; total assimilation of both Marxism and Christianity, dividing up the planes on which each was valid; a proletarian-based messianism.

It is difficult to ascertain whether each and every formulation was or was not correct from the viewpoint of faith, and that question is irrelevant for our purposes here. It is even more difficult to determine whether the impact of dangers, attitudes, and institutional modifications weighed more than that of correct formulas. But what is certain is that the Roman Curia condemned and suppressed many books, articles, and reviews that were considered "progressivist." And it is difficult to determine to what extent Vatican II really rehabilitated the people involved, their experiences and findings, and their theoretical formulas.

The important thing for us here, however, is to see how one of the most important French theologians, Gaston Fessard, found a basis in traditional Christian spirituality for condemning the most solid and perhaps most decisive argument of the progressivist movement: i.e., deliberately opting for a better future.[8]

Starting right from the conflict between the synagogue and Christianity and following the latter through its confrontations with historical revolutions, we see that the defenders of the old order close themselves to dialogue with new values. And there seems to be a basic law in this process of closure that operates outside of authentic Christianity. It is the new values, the ones that seem hostile to Christianity, that ultimately give new life and blood to the Christian message. The "new Christians" knock at the door from without.

Here is how Fessard presents the progressivist argument, which he will later refute: "Let us accept what Mounier and Montuclard say. Let us admit that today's bourgeois Christians stand over against the Communists as the Christianity of the *Ancien Regime* stood over against the French revolutionaries and as the Jews stood over against the gentiles. One can then logically lay stress on the eventual good will of the Communists despite their atheism, and on the possible pharisaism of the bourgeois despite their membership in the Church. There is then the prospect that tomorrow the former will end up converted pagans and the latter incredulous Jews. And it is a short step from there to the conclusion that the world of the pagans will soon occupy the place of the rejected pharisees." [9]

Not without reason Fessard right away points out that the force of this argument is based on the constant repetition of certain historical phenomena. Or, to put it in other words, it is based on the notion of an evolutionary process wherein a certain dialectic enables us to opt for what we can foresee *will be* the best solution: i.e., the solution that is closest to or least alienated from the Christian ideal: "*My option* is already made by the mere *adoption* of an outlook in which the uncertainty and indeterminateness of the future has disappeared, to be replaced by the inevitableness and necessity of a natural event that is foreseeable on natural grounds." [10]

But at this point a suspicious stress begins to appear in Fessard's argument. It is clear enough that historical foreseeability implies some kind of necessary relationship between the present and the future. But it seems equally true that the option against this viewpoint implies the same thing, if we are to judge from the way that the conservative camp reacts to the progressivist camp. What is more, this necessary relationship is not one of absolute necessity at all; it is one of probability. Thus it does not exclude personal liberty or community liberty, the arena *par excellence* in which God's grace is operative. If you will, it is not pure "horizontalism" which rules out any and all "verticality" or transcendence.

How then does one attack the progressivist option in favor of historical foreseeability? One does so by claiming that verticality and transcendence show up only in the total absence of forseeability: i.e., only in pure immobilism. There, and only there, is God's will encountered and his transcendence respected.

This is what Fessard has to say about the basic argument of the progressivists: "Serious as this flaw is from the viewpoint of reason, it is even more serious from the standpoint of faith. If faith is going to shed light on my present . . . the first thing I must do is to blot out any prospect for the future, anything that would claim to decide this future in the name of some merely human law of history that would be *a fortiori* natural . . . But it is not enough to empty oneself completely of any certainty about the future. To make this emptiness complete and at the same time imbue it with supernatural light, I must perceive this *later on,* looming right ahead of me, as possibly being the terminus of my personal history. Or, to put it in purely formal terms, I must perceive it as possibly being the last *later on,* with no *later on* behind it" [11]

Right at this point Fessard tries to show that only this way of recognizing God's will in history dovetails with Christian spirituality. And to do this he makes use of three hypothetical examples which Saint Ignatius proposes in his *Spiritual Exercises.* When a person is faced with some option in history, Ignatius suggests that three hypothetical situations may help him to decide what to choose: 1. Picture some human being whom you have never seen or known, but whom you want to reach his or her fullest perfection; ponder what you would tell this person to choose and do in this particular situation. 2. Pretend you are at the point of death, and then imagine what manner and form you would like this present choice to have taken. 3. Imagine yourself on the day of judgment, and consider how you then would like to have deliberated about your present option (see *Spritual Exercises,* sec. 185–187).

Bypassing the first hypothetical case, Fessard feels that the second and third cases confirm his own thesis that an option is all the more supernatural when it is cut off from any connection with some future we desire to construct within history: "In his *Spiritual Exercises,* which represent a universal method of decision-making, St. Ignatius specifically recommends that we consider our death at the moment of choosing . . . and then the Last Judgment. If we do otherwise, are we really taking Christ seriously when he warns us that the Son of Man will come as a thief? . . . Thus the second coming of Christ, the Parousia, is the happening-type whose light illuminates the dark recesses of the future even as his first coming, the Incarnation, enables me to judge the past." [12]

Whatever traces of immoblism may exist in the theology of the *Spritual Exercises,* belonging as it does to the sixteenth century, it is clear that Fessard misconstrues the obvious point of the latter two examples. As their content clearly indicates, the aim of focusing one's attention on his death and the final judgment is not to exclude consideration and evaluation of the future and its foreseeable course. Quite the contrary is true. The aim is to make sure that our consideration and evaluation of the future is done without reservation or compromise or considerations of self-interest (hence the first example); that instead it will serve as the vehicle for some absolute value (which death and judgment symbolize for the Christian).

Two things show up quite clearly in Fessard's formulation of the problem. The prevailing spirituality lacked an evolutionary viewpoint with which to understand the gospel. Lacking this viewpoint, it lived the gospel as if God's presence in history were all the more clear insofar as it was free of "human calculations," all the more "supernatural" insofar as our intention was directed vertically to God and less interested in influencing results in the future, all the more "absolute" insofar as it was bound up with the present moment. What is more, this present moment which is supposed to orientate our option toward God's vertical presence in our "here and now" could be identified and equated with all the sacralizations of the status quo. Only these sacralizations point to something sacred that is present here and now.

And we must add one more point. The impact of this spirituality goes far beyond the boundaries of the Christian faith. In more secularized forms it pervades the whole realm of bourgeois idealism. Hegel created an evolutionary conception that was apparently dialectical to some extent.[13] Not surprisingly, however, he ends up identifying the definitive realization of Absolute Spirit with the real-life State of his own era.[14]

III. STRUCTURAL PASSIVITY

To speak of "law" is to speak of social structures. And yet the characteristic feature of Christian grace and the Christian message is to help us get beyond the plane of law.

What, then, does "get beyond" mean here? The question takes on political overtones when two aspects are set against one another in the process of liberation: (1) Individual liberation (from the law); (2) the transformation of oppressive social structures—i.e., the creation of a new and better "law."

To take but one example of the problem, here is what Paul VI says at one point in, *Octogesima adveniens*: "Today human beings yearn to free themselves from need and from control by outsiders. But this sort of liberation *starts* with interior liberty, which must be regained with regard to one's own possessions and actions . . . Otherwise, as one can plainly see, the most innovative and revolutionary doctrines lead to nothing but a change of masters" (n. 45; our italics). Once again we are faced with a question: How are we to understand this "start"?

Even setting aside the more obviously distorted interpretations of the term, we feel that the word "start" is an unfortunate choice.

The first—and most preposterous—way of interpreting this "start" is one that unfortunately is not clearly ruled out in the context of the passages where it appears. It presupposes that to a certain extent the transformation of structures is *preceded* by the interior conversion which, in fact, is *caused* by the former. In other words, the presupposition is that there is no valid, constructive, "Christian" revolution in history which does not proceed from the interior conviction of the majority of people, if not of all the people affected by it. In this view the Christian conception of revolution is not a conception of revolution at all. In envisions an *evolution*, in the specific sense that individuals situated in one sector of thought and action will gradually mature and shift over to the opposing sector which is a proponent of new structures.

One need only look at history to see that none of the important forward steps taken by humanity—which cannot be labelled a mere "change of masters"—arose in this manner. Consider the creation of Roman law, for example.

But perhaps the most interesting thing to note is that original sin ultimately is the key factor in the failure to perceive and appreciate the role of structural change. And this in itself is quite a paradox. The dogma of original sin is a dogma propounding the "structural" solidarity of the family of man.[15] Yet in this case it is used to deny this "structural" quality and to propound "individual" avoidance of sin. Sin, it is assumed, becomes a general thing by the addition of one sinning individual to another.

What else could one mean when one says that liberation "starts" with interior liberty? There is another interpretation which, obvious as it may seem, does not fit in with the context. Obviously enough every movement for liberation is born in the conscious awareness of an individual or a small group already liberated enough to propose a new society and new structures for it. Equally obvious, however, is the fact that the Pope's apostolic letter is not thinking of this. This would be a *de facto* condition: there is no profound change that does not begin with an interior liberation (of some individual or of some small group). But *Octogesima adveniens* is talking about a *de jure* condition: i.e., about a generalized quality that must exist *if structural transformation is not to be merely a change of masters*. Hence this is not the correct interpretation of the papal text. But if it were, it would entail another dangerous type of ignorance about evolution in history, this one too propounded in the name of original sin.

The fact is that if this "start" is to be specifically Christian in character, it must be a continuing thing. In other words, criticism must start anew at every moment. And here again we see that a continuing process of starting over before the movement consolidates and becomes a mass phenomenon is a constant source of restraint impeding substantial change. There would not even be a change of masters. Here we have a key to understanding the rejection of the historical dialectic with its "hour of the masses" and its movement through "the dictatorship of the proletariat" and so forth.

The most favorable interpretation of the "start" here would seem to entail the following affirmations: (a) interior conversion, the liberation of minorities, is the theoretical starting point for structural liberative praxis; (b) interior conversion is not the cause of structural change, it simply collaborates in a movement where mass lines of conduct are indispensable for achieving change; (c) if mass lines of conduct are not to oversimplify the new structures and turn them into new enslaving molds with new masters, they must always be complemented by minorities that are interiorly converted and hence more liberated from mass mechanisms; (d) assuming that a deeply lived Christianity is this latter element involved in structural change, its efficacy—which is always a requirement—will vary with the *phases* of the liberative process, and it will have to accept these variations as conditions surrounding a realistic liberation.

Taking these factors into account, one can say that the leaven of Christianity is indeed important and indispensable if structual transformations are not to stop with a mere change of masters. But the word *start* seems singularly ill chosen and open to much ambiguity. It would have been much more logical to talk about a "necessary complementarity." But the language and mentality of the Church, still reluctant to open up to an evolutionary perspective, seems to be in search of some framework in which Christianity is the only party possessing the means to achieve the desired goal, which it will achieve *alone*. In line with this outlook, it equates this means with interior liberation. It sees interior liberation as the *cause* of authentic liberation in its totality, which would include structural liberation.

And so from one generation to the next, Christian *passivity* becomes increasingly patent. Christianity keeps waiting and hoping, expecting that each and every individual human being will grasp the well-founded point of the gospel's demands and that new societies will ultimately arise from this universal consensus.

IV. THE AMBIVALENCE OF SATAN AND SIN IN THE BIBLE

Many Christians believe that God's test of his angels, Lucifer's rebellion and the subsequent fall of himself and his supporters to a place of torment, and their continuing effort since then to snatch man's destiny from God's hands, are part of divine revelation. That is not the case.[16]

In the whole Bible we do not find the slightest trace of an Anti-God, an autonomous principle of evil. To be sure, temptations are described metaphorically in human terms: someone whispers a sinful proposal into a person's ear. But any attempt to take these passages literally is rejected by the Epistle of James: "No one under trial or temptation should say, 'I am being tempted by God'; for God is untouched by evil, and does not himself tempt anyone. Temptation arises when a man is enticed and lured away by his own lust; then lust [here meaning "concupiscence"] conceives, and gives birth to sin; and sin full-grown breeds death" (Jas. 1:13–15). [17]

Now if Satan does not show up as a God of evil, what exactly is his relationship to Yahweh? On the one hand his relationship with evil seems clear. On the other hand his subordination to the one and only Lord of history seems equally obvious. And it is interesting to note that in the field of exegesis the term *dialectic* has arisen to define this sort of relationship.[18]

In broad outlines the biblical development of the notion of Satan and his functions in the Old Testament might be spelled out this way. Even though it is difficult to pinpoint exact points in time here, it does seem that the Hebrew writers avoided associating Yahweh directly with certain divine interventions even before the sacred name of God was proscribed from written texts. Yahweh was their author, to be sure, but through the mediate intervention of an "angel" or a "messenger" (cf. Gen. 16; Exod. 3; and so forth).

Now since Yahweh was regarded as the one and only source of everything that happened to man, be it beneficial or harmful, it was only logical that the dissociation mentioned above came into play all the more when the events in question brought adversity to man. And this was especially true when they struck people who were personally innocent (note the exterminating "angel" of 1 Chron. 21:14–15; and the "evil spirit from God" of 1 Sam. 18:10).

It is important for us to remember that the Old Testament outlook was that even these dire happenings were *necessary* in God's salvific plan. But as time passed and their notion of God was refined, the biblical writers were more and more reluctant to attribute these necessary evils *directly* to Yahweh as the Yahwist account had done in describing the extermination of Egypt's first-born (cf. Exod. 12). More and more these functions, which are *necessary* and remain under Yahweh's direction, are carried out by "persons." Or, to put it more clearly, they are turned into "personalized functions" so as to dissociate them stylistically from Yahweh the beneficent.

Now among these "personalized functions" there appears *Satan,* who ever remains subordinate to Yahweh and his plans (cf. 1 Chron. 21:1; Job 1:6 ff; and so forth).

Note that we are not explaining what Satan is *in se*. We are explaining how the idea of God evolved in divine revelation and thereby led to a conception of Satan that differs greatly from ours.

The process itself is significant. The historical process is one, and it is directed by Yahweh himself toward the fulfillment of his promises. Within this process evil does not proceed from another God nor does it belie Yahweh's benevolence. It is a necessary part of the process, and hence it merits epithets that take due account of its ambiguous—or better, dialectical—role: the same process is due to Yahweh and to Satan. It is as if God had to deploy mechanisms of mass justice on the one hand while on the other hand he goes about fulfilling his plan of personalizing love with their help.[19] As we have seen many times before, this kind of language would be contradictory in any line of thought that was not evolutionary or dialectical.

It is not easy to sum up in a few words what the satanic, the demonic, signifies in the New Testament. Depending on their respective points of view, the various New Testament authors stress one or another feature.

John, for example, talks about the "prince of this world." In dealing with the devil, his Gospel frames him within the categories we have studied in connection with the term *world*. This term *world* is a key notion in John's theology, and we have tried to indicate the wealth of meaning it contains.

But we must say something about the demonic in the Synoptic Gospels and about "sin" in Saint Paul's writings.

One of the most suggestive treatments of the demonic in the Synoptic Gospels is found in an episode that is disconcerting at first glance. It concerns the liberation of the Gerasene man who had been possessed by a host of demons (Mark 5:1ff; Matt. 8:28 ff; Luke 8:26 ff.). Here we are not interested in the "historical" reality of the demonic possession and the course it took. What we want to do is to look at the account and note the traits that the Jewish religious outlook associated with the devil's presence and activity.

And here again we do not find any of the diabolic characteristics that we spontaneously associate with the devil: e.g., a cold-blooded, rebel spirit. If these creatures are devils, they are "poor devils." [20]

Not foreseeing the disgrace they will suffer, these devils rush to encounter Jesus. They recognize him as the Son of God, adore him, beg him not to torment them, and obey his mandate. But they also reveal a trait unheard of in rebel spirits: they are terrorized by the prospect of having to leave the region, their favorite haunt, and so they ask Jesus to allow them to possess a different set of bodies—even though the latter are irrational swine and even though they cannot induce them to commit anything resembling sin.

The very fact that all this is done with the permission of the Lord would seem to suggest further that possession itself is subject to God's will. And this is akin to the way John's Gospel explains a man's blindness

from birth: "It is not that this man or his parents sinned . . . He was born
blind so that God's power might be displayed in curing him" (John 9:3).
In short, it is a necessary part of God's beneficent plan, but it is attributed to God's "executors" rather than directly to God himself.

What is more, few passages in the Synoptic Gospels present us with
such a clear picture of "God's power" at work as the story of the
Gerasene man does. Here we see what liberation from diabolic possession means. If we compare the "before" and "after," we find the following features. *Before* the man moves around purposelessly, has no human
domicile, makes inarticulate cries, suffers to no good purpose, and has
brutal strength but does no positive work. *After* he displays common
sense, is capable of speech and dialogue and tranquillity, and can look
for a proper social function.

In other words the demonic in the gospel is not the temptation that
follows man's full development; it is the prehuman, presocial stage from
which Christ and his followers are commissioned to free man. Man is in
bondange to a power: the kingdom of Satan. Jesus fights against this
power and disarms it. But instead of substituting his own brand of enslavement for that of Satan, he "divides the plunder" which the latter
had taken from humanity; thus human beings can be truly human once
again (cf. Mark 3:22–27; Matt. 12:22–29; and especially Luke 11:14–22).

We can put this another way. In the Synoptic Gospels the satanic
element does not show up as an independent force for evil. It shows up
as the base—negative but necessary—on which the humanizing power of
God will build. God's power dominates the process from first to last,
leading it to its ultimate fulfillment in which the powerful work of God
will be manifested *in it*.

Naturally enough Paul's thinking on sin is more fully worked out, but
it does not lose its radical ambiguity for all that. There is a clear convergence between John's world–hour dialectic and Paul's law–sin dialectic.

To begin with, we must point out that Paul generally uses two terms
which we today translate as "sin." One term (*parábasis,* or *hamartíai* in the
plural) refers to transgressions against the law, to what we would call
voluntary sins. The other term (*hamartía* in the singular) has two senses
in Greek; it means "deviation" (i.e., "missing the mark") or "sin." This is
the term that interests us here. We shall simply translate it as "sin."

Now this "sin" tyrannizes humanity as a whole. In the Epistle to the
Romans, a key document in Paul's and Christian thinking on sin, Paul
says this: "Jew and Greek alike are all under the power of sin" (Rom.
3:9). This means that "all human beings" are under the power of sin,
because the use of paired opposites (Jew and Greek, circumcised and
uncircumcised, and so forth) is a biblical way of designating the totality.

This climate of oppression and this state of dependency and bondage
show up constantly in Paul's writings: "You, who once were slaves of sin,
have yielded whole-hearted obedience to the pattern of teaching to

which you were made subject, and emancipated from sin . . . " (Rom.
6:17). Obviously enough they have not been emancipated from "sins,"
since they still commit them, as Paul's frequent admonitions indicate. A
few verses later Paul again stresses the same point: "When you were
slaves of sin . . . But now, freed from the commands of sin . . . " (Rom.
6:20,22).

It begins to dawn on us that "sin" is different from the "sins" that
come from freely made choices. Sin is a condition that subdues and
enslaves me against my own will. It is a part of my being, the most basic
and low-level part if not the most profound and authentic part (which is
why I am "enslaved"). It sustains me and yet at the same time prevents
me from being the human person I desire to be.

In the next chapter Paul goes on to say: "The good which I want to
do, I fail to do; but what I do is the wrong which is against my will' (Rom.
7:19). It is a state of dissociation, dispossession, alienation. We are subject to an alien power. And this is Paul's explanation for it: "If what I do
is against my will, clearly it is no longer I who am the agent, but sin that
has its lodging in me" (Rom. 7:20). Where precisely is the lodging place
of this sin that takes over my actions? Paul, making use of a comparison
that exemplifies what happens in each individual human being, locates it
in *the structure* of his own being which follows its own law: "I perceive that
there is in my bodily members a different law, fighting against the law
that my reason approves and making me a prisoner under the law that is
in my members, the law of sin" (Rom. 7:23).

This law of our bodily members, governing our basic low-level structure, is something that Paul will extend to the structures of our social
being in other passages (cf. Gal. 3:28; 1 Cor. 12:13). The important
point here is that sin in Paul's writings, like the demonic in the Synoptic
Gospels and the world in John's Gospel, becomes an equivocal and ambiguous thing insofar as it is dissociated from transgressions against the
law and linked up with the fulfillment of a law that is below the level of
total human fulfillment, that is not absolutely bad but not absolutely
good either: "It was sin that killed me, and thereby sin exposed its true
character; it used a good thing . . . the commandment [of the law]"
(Rom. 7:13).

So once again we see something that we have seen before. When we
are trying to evaluate such apparently negative terms as sin and the
devil, we find that an *unequivocal* interpretation does not do justice to the
rich thought of Scripture. Even its most primitive literary devices and
genres suggest an *ambivalence* that calls for an evolutionary and dialectical viewpoint.

NOTES

1. It would be interesting to explore to what extent Christians do or do not take it for granted that divine redemption reaches all men equally, without any restrictions. To give one suggestive example, here is what the "progressive" Jean Mouroux writes in one of his books: "In spite of the original transgression everything still bears the divine imprint . . . All is redeemed in Christ *in principle*" (our italics; Jean Mouroux, *The Meaning of Man*, Eng. trans. by A.H.G. Downes, New York: Sheed & Ward, 1952, p. 8). The last two words are typical. No one would dare to say that original sin has been efficacious *in principle*.

2. Marx, "Le communisme de 'L'Observateur rhénan'," in the *Gazette Allemande de Bruxelles*, n. 73, September 12, 1847.

3. Paul VI, Apostolic letter on the eightieth anniversary of the encyclical *Rerum novarum, Octogesima adveniens*, n. 26; *The Pope Speaks* magazine, Washington, D.C., 16:150. The apostolic letter is dated May 14, 1971.

4. *Sertum laeticiae*, n. 14. To be sure, Pius XII adds that God does not want this inequality to degenerate into the oppression of one group by the other. But what if we look at the problem of rich and poor *social classes* rather than at rich and poor individuals in isolation! Doesn't the unequal class situation itself constitute an unjust oppression?

5. Encyclical *Ad Beatissimi*, n. 10.

6. Leo XIII, *Rerum novarum*, n. 12. See also Pius XI, *Divini Redemptoris*, n. 7. In the latter text Pius XI applies the label *paradise* (with its welter of theological overtones) to a society in which "each would give according to his ability and receive according to his needs." Later on we shall point out some of the excessively utopian connotations in the picture of a rectilinear evolution of society. See Chapter V, CLARIFICATION III.

7. See Volume I, Chapter I, CLARIFICATION II; Volume II, Chapter II, especially Section III of the main article and CLARIFICATION II.

8. Even though Fessard takes a negative stance toward this tendency, his two volumes give us a good picture of the main outlines of the "progressive" movement. The ideas and documents gathered there provide an interesting prelude to some present-day problems. See Gaston Fessard, *De l'actualité historique* (Paris: Desclée, 1959), in two volumes.

9. *Ibid.*, II, 63.

10. *Ibid.*, II, 64.

11. *Ibid.*, pp. 64–65.

12. *Ibid.*, p. 65.

13. Marx would say that this dialectic had to be set back on its feet again before it could move forward again.

14. It is worth noting that in France Fessard represents a theology based on a philosophical methodology derived directly from Hegel.

15. Because even after divine redemption it continues to "structure" majority attitudes with its permanent *tendency*.

16. The origin of this story is to be found in a combination of passages from Isaiah and Daniel: "How you have fallen from heaven, bright morning star, felled to the earth, sprawling helpless across the nations! You thought in your own mind, I will scale the heavens . . . Yet you shall be brought down to Sheol"

(Isa. 14:12–15); "It cast down to the earth some of the host and some of the stars and trod them underfoot" (Dan 8:10). The only thing is that both prophecies refer to human political events expressed in metaphors. One (Isa. 14:4–21) refers to the death of a tyrant while the other (Dan 8:20 ff.) refers to the fate of an eastern king along with all rebels.

17. These last words (along with those that refer to the origin of sin) are important because they explain the sense in which we should interpret such statements as the following one in John's Gospel: "Your father is the *devil* and you choose to carry out your father's desires. He was a *murder* from the beginning . . . " (John 8:44). The devil that causes death is the sequence spelled out in James' Epistle: man's own lust, sin, death.

18. Riwkah Schärf, "La figura de Satanás en el Antiguo Testamento," in C. G. Jung, *Simbología del Espíritu* (Spanish trans. by Rodríguez Cabo, México: FCE, 1962), p. 147; original title in German, *Symbolik des Geistes*, Zurich, 1953). Our statements here borrow freely from that article.

19. Adolphe Lods makes this pointed comment about the Old Testament conception of Satan: "Thus *satan* here represents . . . strict law, which in a given case stands in opposition to Yahweh's merciful plan. It is justice in conflict with grace" ("Les origines de la figure de Satan," cited by Schärf, *ibid.*, p. 213.

20. The Synoptic Gospels do not present Satan thus except for the episode about Christ's temptation in the desert (Matt. 4:1–11; Luke 4:1–13), but the latter is in a different literary genre. What is more, exegetes tend to interpret this episode along the lines of Dostoyevsky's insightful presentation of it in *The Brothers Karamazov*. They tend to regard these temptations, not as a conflict between one spirit and another spirit, but rather as a potential *distortion* of Jesus' salvific vocation into a mass-directed one. This would accord with what we say here—aside from the difference in literary genre noted above.

CHAPTER FOUR

Sin at the Origin of Evolution

In the two preceding chapters we attempted to establish two bridgeheads that might serve to bring together the notions of "evolution" and "guilt." On the one hand we looked at the law of entropy and found therein an element of evolution analogous to guilt. As evolution advances toward the realm of liberty and societal organization, this element shows up ever more clearly as guilt. It is always something prior, something from the past; and at the same time it is an essential part of every human life and every human society. On the other hand we looked at the biblical conception of guilt. And we found that it entailed much more than the concrete decision of an individual human being and his liberty. It seemed to point toward a structure, a structure that is clearly social and evolutionary. In its lower stages this structure was intertwined with the very base of all life, all liberty, and hence all redemption; and the base, in itself, was not sinful.

In the two chapters that remain we shall try to move from each of these solid foundations toward the other.

Section I

From its earliest days the Christian Church has been confronted with a certitude and a doubt—both present in a confused way in the writings of Paul himself. In the Epistle to the Romans, indeed in the same sentence, we find two notions: "It was *through one man* that sin entered the world, and through sin death, and thus death pervaded the whole human race, *inasmuch as all men have sinned*" (Rom. 5:12; our italics). Here we find a certainty: sin and death (the consequence of sin) are the common lot of *all* humanity. And we find an ambiguity: in the sentence and its surrounding context this condition is attributed to *a single sin* (cf. Rom. 5:15,17,18,19) and to the sin *of all* (cf. Rom. 5:16,19,20).[1]

We can say that this ambiguity, viewed as a dilemma in its static terms, was the basis for all the controversies concerning "original" sin that took place in the Church from the fifth to the sixteenth century.

As early as 418 the Council of Carthage had to fight against those who drew the logical conclusion from the fact that sin was a deviation resulting from man's free will. They maintained that a human being, by the mere fact of being born, could not have any sin that demanded pardon. In other words, they maintained that the sin "of one man" could not be transmitted physically or genetically. If sin did reign in the world, it was *because* (or, inasmuch as)[2] "all sinned." This would obviously leave out those who were incapable of sin as yet: i.e., children who had not yet reached the age of reason.

This opinion was condemned (Denz. 102). And from that point on Christian dogma would insist on two basic points every time that the problem came up again: 1. *The propagation of the human species,* not any individual act, is the mainspring for the transmission of this sin (Denz. 790; cf. Denz. 109, 175, 711, 795); 2. Despite the nature of the transmission, it is a *real sin* in each and every human being and not merely a punishment for the fault of another situated in the past (Denz. 789 and 792; cf. Denz. 175, 376, 532, 795).

But the force and persistent emphasis of this twofold affirmation in no way explains or clarifies the compatibility of the terms: i.e., something *physical* producing a *moral* evil, propagation communicating sin.

In other words the notion of sin itself must assume broader dimensions than it is usually given if we want to be able to apply it to a human situation in which free consent does not exist.[3] At the same time, however, the word *sin* would be emptied of all meaning if it were to be dissociated from the realm of "the voluntary" (Denz. 1046–1047). In such a case its effect would be magical in character. It would be totally alien to man's interior life and hence incapable of closing him off from his one, supreme, vocation: personal dialogue with God (GS 19 and 22).

Hence we must situate this "sin" of all humanity *midway* between the nascent realm of volition and freely deliberated decision. Once again we may point out that even though this dogma is expressed in static terms, it points toward some sort of evolution; otherwise its words would say exactly the opposite of what they do say.[4]

Now if all that is true, is there really such a radical difference as some people claim between this sin of humanity and concupiscence? The usual statement is that original sin has been "blotted out" by Christ's redemptive work; that all that remains, so to speak, is a tendency to evil which we can resist.[5]

Here we find a juridical conception of sin and its consequences, and of redemption and its consequences, which fits in very neatly with a static presentation such as that of Trent. Juridically speaking, and without any coherent explanation of the fact being offered, the claim is that man is responsible for a sin that he personally has not committed, a sin in which any possibility of free consent is ruled out (cf. Denz. 532). This "injustice" perpetrated on each and every human individual is remedied by a redemption which is pictured as a possibility to which the individual may have recourse: i.e., the individual's "guilt" can be blotted out by Christ's merits. The moment he does this (i.e., receives baptism), what was really and truly sin in him is destroyed in the same external, juridical manner in which it arrived "so that as a result there is absolutely nothing that can delay his entrance into heaven" (Denz. 792).

One inexplicable fact remains, however. The juridico–biological element which produces the situation of sin appears to be more powerful than the juridico–salvific element engendered by redemption. The "involuntary" sin introduced guilt and *consequences* into man. Redemption erased only the guilt. It did not choose, or *was not able,* to erase the consequences. Concupiscence continues to be part of redeemed man's basic human condition.

Saint Paul did not think this way when he declared that grace had overcome sin in itself and *in its consequences* (Rom. 5:12–20).

Correct as it may be in its general form, isn't the juridical formulation inadequate when it comes to informing us of a reality that is more dynamic and communitarian than its terms can handle? Once again we are led to ask: Is there really such a radical difference between sin and concupiscence as this juridical language insinuates?

The Council of Trent itself had to admit openly that it was departing from the language of Paul in using this juridical distinction. In other words, it was departing from the language of divine revelation itself, which applies the term "sin" both to sin itself and to concupiscence (sin as a tendency; cf. Denz. 792).[6]

Let us take the critical elements we have just indicated and connect them with other elements that point in an even more positive way toward what might be a coherent understanding of divine redemption. The fact is that redemption is the *reality* that enables us to understand and appreciate the original sin *overcome* by it, contrary to our usual way of looking at the matter. It is not the visible *fact* of original sin triumphant that informs us about some possible liberation in which we must simply *believe* despite the fact that everything we see in history seems to belie that possibility. Quite the contrary is true. Our human history is the concrete history of a redeemed humanity in which only faith can enlighten us about an authentic *sin* situated at our common origin. Our concrete experience, which only runs up against the *tendency* to evil, cannot do this.

Let us look at the two complementary elements of this redemption in Christ. From the start *divine redemption was viewed as liberation.* Even though the very word "redeem" was part of the juridical vocabulary of Rome, it never signified the mere act of declaring a guilty party innocent, of pardoning or erasing his sin. It signified the legal process of restoring an enslaved person to freedom and paying the required price to that end.

In this connection it is quite interesting to read and ponder the text where Paul, according to Trent, calls "sin" what he should have more precisely called "concupiscence" (i.e., what remains of sin after it has been wiped out as sin). Paul says: "Sin must no longer reign in your mortal body, exacting obedience to the body's desire . . . Sin shall no longer be your master, because you are no longer under law, but under the grace of God . . . When you were slaves of sin, you were free from the control of righteousness" (Rom. 6:12,14,20).

It is Paul who introduces into Scripture the theme of an original sin propagated to the whole human race, and he does so in the Epistle to the Romans. But it is this same Paul, writing in the same epistle, who presents the redemptive work of grace as a liberation. The dominant theme is the passage from slavery to liberty. Even though the term *sin* often shows up as the subject of a verbal phrase, the process is never presented as a passage from sin to pardon, from sin to innocence, from sin to fulfillment of the law. It is not even presented as a passage from sin to love. The change involved is a passage from the *enslavement* of sin (i.e., from a state where it is impossible not to sin) to the *possibility* of loving despite the power of sin. This power of sin remains, but it is no longer totally dominant.[7]

It is interesting and highly significant for us to consider why this passage, which refers constantly to sin, is interpreted by Trent as referring strictly to *concupiscence* only. The obvious reason is that the whole passage presents sin as something that can be overcome. If that is the case, then it cannot be referring to original sin (an unfailing situation of sin); it must be referring to concupiscence (a situation in which we struggle against the tendency to sin). In other words, what redemption has achieved with respect to one and the same force, sin, is to enable us to pass from the irresistible dominion of this force to the possibility of fighting against it and overcoming it.[8]

This supports us in our hypothesis that original sin and concupiscence, so separated from the viewpoint of morality, would be completely interfused and confounded with each other if divine redemption had not sparked in man the possibility of resisting this single force.

Hence we can draw the conclusion that redemption did not erase original sin *totally*, insofar as it let the tendency to sin remain.[9] What it did erase was the enslavement: i.e., the radical impossibility of man's exercising his human liberty vis-à-vis sin and grace. In other words, it made a true human being out of everyone who belonged biologically to the human race by procreation. Man, as a human being, was now capable of dialoguing personally with God and his fellow men and thereby attaining eternal life (Denz. 410 and 791).

From the way divine revelation and the Church's magisterium express it, it is clear that one force shifts from being a determining force to being a determinable force. *Another force* is at work in us, so that we can shift from being enslaved beings to being humans who are now capable of fighting against evil. And this latter force redeems us so that we might be human beings.

In the juridical language mentioned earlier, the tendency to evil seemed to be the defeat of grace vis-à-vis the condition of sin. In the other language discussed here, the tendency to evil shows up as the victory of a grace that wanted us to take personal hold over our own destiny.

And in this second language we again see that the force of redemption is akin to the whole force of evolution at work in the distinct and successive thresholds which the universe has passed. The same forces continue to be operative. The same inclination—associated with entropy—continues to operate in favor of facile syntheses and enslavement to repetition and quantitative majorities. Yet, despite this inclination, life continues to move above it and to head for new possibilities: negentropy. Life continues to move toward more difficult but attainable potentialities where what was dominant before is dominated to some extent; and then it stops there on a new threshold, while the process is repeated.

Section II

But there is an argument against this position which is not inconsiderable and must be noted. The fact is that the Church's magisterium, grounded in an age-old tradition and apparently in revelation itself (through Paul's texts), presents Christ's redemption as God's rectification of a plan in which man's sin figured *only as a possibility:* "Almighty

God created man upright, without sin, and with free will. He placed him in paradise and wanted him to remain in holiness and righteousness. Man, using his free will wrongly, sinned and fell . . . We lost the liberty of our free will in the first man, and we recover it through Christ our Lord" (Council of Quiercy in 853, Denz., 316–317; cf. Denz. 788, 2328).

Wherein lies the force of this argument? It lies in three points. It puts an *historical* difficulty, a *juridical* difficulty, and a *theological* difficulty in the way of our explanation in Section I.

The historical difficulty does not lie really in the account of Adam's sin in the Book of Genesis, because nowhere in the Old Testament does his sin appear to become automatic and formally sinful for all humanity. The historical difficulty lies in the fact that Paul attributes the universal propagation of sin to this "historical" sin of Adam. *After* the Epistle to the Romans, in other words, the Genesis narrative of Adam's sin appears to be the narrative of the original sin itself.[10]

Now if original sin could be dated historically, then it seems undeniable that the first datum of history would not be man's enslavement and his subsequent emergence into liberty through redemption. The first man would have originally existed in a state of liberty and righteousness. And this state hardly resembles the state of the primitive human being that the science of evolution attempts to present to us.

In considering this whole issue it is most important that we frame the statements of the magisterium in their proper historical context. Until very recently Christian certainty about the infallibility of God's revelation in Scripture was erroneously extended to the whole of its written content. No notice was taken of the various literary genres in Scripture and their differing relationships to the truth (Denz. 2294). It was not until 1950 that the magisterium took the latter factors into account and established certain exegetical principles as common church teaching: "The first eleven chapters of Genesis admittedly do not accord with the methods of historical writing that are followed . . . by scholars in our day. But in a real sense, and it is up to exegetes to explore and spell out this sense more precisely, they do belong to the genre of history. In a simple and figurative way these chapters do contain . . . both the principle truths on which eternal salvation is based, and a popular description of the origin of the human race" (Denz. 2329).

It should not surprise us, then, that earlier documents of the magisterium spoke about Adam's sin as if it—and its conditions and consequences—were something historically documented. So today we can and must reckon with those features that are due to an earlier historical context now corrected by new data.

Now if we do not interpret the account of Adam's sin as an "historical document" in the modern sense of the word,[11] then we can no longer present it as an argument against tying sin and evolution together. Nor can we picture redemption as a new twist of the rudder, as an intervention that is as precisely dated and marked in history as Adam's sin. It is certainly true that Christ's death and resurrection—the latter, for the Christian at least—are historical events with dates and documentation. But no one can look to Christian faith for support for the claim that man's ability to overcome the power of sin *starts from that date* (Denz. 160 b).

The importance of this point will be made clear later. Right now let us move on to the *juridical* difficulty. It would appear that original sin is simply turned into concupiscence. In other words, it shifts from being enslavement to being a struggle, and redemption in turn is bound up with a "juridical" instrument that makes it efficacious: namely, baptism, (Denz. 102, 109 a, 348, 790–792).

Obviously the existence of some "juridical" prerequisite for the attainment of redemption would rule out any evolutionary conception of redemption, and hence of original sin. But the plain fact is that the existence of such a magical, juridical prerequisite does not dovetail with divine revelation.[12] Divine revelation does not talk about any theoretical victory. It talks about the concrete, practical, efficacious victory of redemption over sin, of Christ's work over Adam's work, insofar as all of humanity is concerned. One would be engaging in contradiction to affirm this victory on the one hand, while claiming on the other hand that sin is passed along to all men without any juridical prerequisite whereas grace does call for such a prerequisite and is therefore restricted to an infinitesimal portion of humanity.

What is more, we can look to the recent council here. Vatican II was the first ecumencical council that looked with interest and sympathy on the fate of humanity *as a whole.* It did not restrict its attention to Christians, and on repeated occasions it corrected this legalistic conception of redemption. This is particularly evident in the following statement: "Since Christ died for all men, and since the ultimate vocation of man *is in fact one,* and divine, *we ought to believe* that the Holy Spirit in a manner known only to God offers to *every man* the possibility of being associated with this paschal mystery [i.e., of redemption]" (GS 22; our italics).[13]

Thus if the whole of humanity in every age has received from the Holy Spirit the capacity to escape the enslavement of sin, then we must renounce something: not the concept of original sin, but the presumption that we can meet up with it concretely in history. Our world is a redeemed world and it always was. This does not mean that original sin loses its importance or its truth. It is the truth about what our origins would have been if an opposite force—redemptive grace—had not been placed in man's hands.

And that brings us to the third difficulty, which is specifically and properly *theological*. If what we said is right, then man did not interrupt God's plan. Redemption was not a remedy that God came up with when his original plan was shattered.

There was a theological viewpoint that did see redemption as such a remedy. And even though this viewpoint did not constitute a dogma, it became a very solid tradition through Thomism. During the Middle Ages two schools of theology debated and disagreed over a question that might seem quite hypothetical and idle: Would Christ have come if man had not sinned? The school of Thomas Aquinas answered "no";[14] the school of Duns Scotus answered "yes."

The lapse of time since then, the development of the theology of the Incarnation, and advances in biblical exegesis have enabled us to better gauge and appreciate the arguments of the Scotist school.[15]

The Epistle to the Hebrews (2:10) and the Epistle to the Colossians (1:15–17) tell us that the whole universe was made *for* Christ. This means that Christ the Redeemer is the decisive force that pervades and directs the entire world: human beings, animals, plants, matter. The work of Christ does not begin somewhere along the line: e.g., with the start of humanity. Right from the start the entire universe was journeying toward Emmanuel, toward God-with-us, toward God identified with our history.

In a passage that can be fully meaningful only in an evolutionary context, the Epistle to the Colossians talks about Christ and depicts the work he carried out and then entrusted to us when it had reached its culmination: "His is the primacy over all created things. . . . the whole universe has been created through him and for him. And he exists before everything, and all things are held together in him" (Col. 1:15–17).

The work performed in achieving man's total liberation was the work which created the universe and which maintains it in eager expectation until hominization culminates with "the liberty and splendour of the children of God" (Rom. 8:19–21).

And so, by scrutinizing the most radical objections—or the most classical ones at least—we arrive at our second conclusion: redemption, like sin, is a *universal* force in the most precise and meaningful sense of the word.[16] The "blood of Christ" carries out its redemptive function from creation to the consummation of the universe (Col. 1:14,20). In other words, it continually fights against entropy, the original quantitative force that brings disruption and degeneration to everything that exists. As liberty looms ever more clearly on the horizon, entropy shows up more and more as sin. It is a sin that comes from the past, that is our sin and at the same time the sin of the human community into which we are born.

The use of reason and human liberty are not instants which mark the start of a different reality, a reality that is innocent so long as it is not used deliberately for evil. Any and all real liberty, however minute it may be, is the keepsake of a prior egotism, of an easy way out that was accepted, of a sin. And this is so because sin is far more primeval that it would have been if it had simply been committed one day by the first human being. It is the very base and foundation for the unity of the human species and for our solidarity with the universe. It is the base of our liberty, which puts up resistance to that liberty. It is the world that makes the Incarnation possible and then tries to suffocate it. It is the flesh of society that needs redemption and flees from it.

If someone thinks that evolution and guilt exclude each other, then that person has not grasped what divine revelation does grasp: i.e., the profundity, the "originality," the visceral complexity of sin. Paradoxical as it may seem, we will not understand and appreciate the decisive nature of guilt if we do not frame it within a process where hominization and redemption operate in the identity of one single history.

NOTES TO CHAPTER FOUR

1. The biblical use of such terms as "the many" and "the multitude" almost always signifies "all" or "the totality." It certainly does here (cf. Rom. 5:12,16,18,19).

2. The condemnation of this opinion is reinforced by the fact that the Latin Vulgate version of the Bible erroneously translates this phrase a different way. Instead of rendering it "*inasmuch* as all sinned," it renders the phrase "*in whom* [i.e., Adam] all sinned." Even then, how is it possible to really *sin* "*in* another"?

3. "Sin is twofold: original and actual. Original sin is that which is contracted without consent" (Denz. 410).

4. In reality one would have to say the same thing of original sin that a priest in the cofessional must say about any fault which is not the result of freely given consent: "But that is *not* a sin!"

5. That is the first impression we get from this passage of Trent: "If someone says that all that which has *the real and proper aspect of sin* is not destroyed by

the grace of our Lord Jesus Christ . . . let him be anathema." Now Trent readily admits that concupiscence remains, and then goes on to say: "it cannot harm those who do not consent to it" (Denz. 792).

6. Trent cites Rom. 6:12 ff.

7. One of the first texts of the magisterium on this topic puts it this way: "Only one who was a slave to sin is set free, and only one who truly had been enslaved to sin before can be said to be redeemed" (Denz. 109 a; cf. Denz. 788 and 815).

8. "The New Testament speaks of the victory of Jesus over sin; he destroys the dominion of Sin and Death. The Christian shares in this victory; and dominion over sin means more than forgiveness. It means that the Christian is not under sin unless he submits himself to it; it means not only that he can be forgiven but also that he can overcome sins . . . How often are Christians unwilling to believe that they have been transformed and that the impossible has become possible? " (John L. McKenzie, S.J., *The Power and the Wisdom*, Milwaukee: Bruce, 1965, p. 122).

9. This seems to be the only possible interpretation of the condemnation voiced by Benedict XII back in the fourteenth century on those who claimed that "in his passion Christ completely wiped out the sin of our first parents" (Denz. 532).

10. To use the terms that theologians use, it is the story of the "originating" original sin. "Originating" is used to distinguish this sin from the original sin "originated" by it in the history of each human being.

11. Those exegetes who accept the premises of *Human generis* (Denz. 2329) and acknowledge that the first eleven chapters of Genesis do belong to the genre of history in a way which "*it is up to exegetes to explore and spell out*," maintain that this "history" is the history of the evolutionary origin of man.

12. Nor with more ancient teachings of the magisterium (see, for example, Denz. 160 b).

13. At what point would this "association" take place? If it is really to reach *all men*, it must go back to the moment of birth at least. Speaking of this moment, and referring to all human beings whether they are baptized or not, Vatican II declares: "From the very circumstance of his origin, man is already invited to converse with God" (GS 19). We cannot picture this as a formal, legalistic invitation; it must be an authentic and efficacious one. And that presupposes victory over original sin.

14. See *S. Th.*, III, q. 1, art. 3.

15. "The Scotist interpretation is in line with the teaching of the Bible. The Incarnation is the ultimate aim of creation, insofar as creatures share in the union of the human and the divine in its highest attainment of perfection. Alongside its redemptive sense, the Incarnation also has this other sense—which indicates it was not decreed by God solely in view of sin. The Incarnation is such a grandiose mystery that it cannot simply be the consequence of sin. Divine wisdom would have displayed a contradiction between means and end if God had wrought such an awesome work simply to annul sin. In that case the greatest of God's works would have been performed because of sin. But God does not work good for the sake of evil; he permits evil for the sake of good. The opposing theory would give too much play to sin. The primary thing willed is good, not evil" (Michael Schmaus, *Teologia Dogmática*. Spanish trans. by García-Drudis,

Madrid: Rialp, 1959, III, 84; this is probably a translation of Schmaus' *Katholische Dogmatik*, which is not available in English as such). See also Pierre Grelot, "Réflexions sur le problème du péché originel," in *Nouvelle Revue Théologique* 89 (1967), p. 481.

16. Because the Incarnation that founds the universe is already a redemptive Incarnation. If it is true that "every synthesis is costly," then redemption is the immanent force in the universe that leads it *systematically* to pay the required price; and this goal is visible at a given moment.

CLARIFICATIONS

I. SIN OF THE WORLD OR ORIGINAL SIN?

At this point the reader can readily see that we could have drawn the same conclusions about the relationship between evolution and guilt without ever mentioning Adam's sin or "original sin."

The fact is that no matter what interpretation we give to the latter term, it does not in the least diminish the force of the arguments establishing an intimate relationship between evolution and sin. At least that is certainly true if we are talking about a sin that is not individual but is proper to the human species as such. To avoid misunderstandings and difficulties, we could have used Schoonenberg's approach and talked about a "sin of the world." [1] We could have shown that its existence is demanded by the very notion of evolution (i.e., a nonmechanistic evolution) and by a whole series of biblical references that are much plainer and more numerous than those which refer specifically to original sin. [2] Then we could have left it up to the reader to decide whether "sin of the world" should or should not be identified with "original sin." It is a moot question much debated by theologians.

This approach would have several advantages. On the one hand we would have been spared the task of presuming to offer an explanation of original sin, and consequently we would not have had to tread our way through the dogmatic niceties that must be considered in talking about the sin. The "sin of the world" is a datum of biblical theology that has not been sufficiently utilized and explored up to now. And it can give a communitarian dimension to grace and sin which is very much in line with Scripture as a whole.

On the other hand the data referring to this "sin of the world" would also have positive value. It would bring out another important point: namely, that an authentic evolutionary view of the universe—of both human history and the stages below it—does not rule out the decisive importance of sin but rather presupposes it. The accusation made against the evolutionary view on the basis of Teilhard de Chardin's works is a false one insofar as it it turned into a general indictment.

87

But in our opinion the disadvantages of adopting the "sin of the world" approach outweigh the advantages. First of all, we have shown that original sin, as embodied in immobilist ideas and images, often constitutes an alienating element in the Christian faith. It takes the heart out of faith when it comes to considering any "structural sin" and turns it into an individualistic thing. Our feeling, however, is that the dogma of original sin is a key to understanding how and why human beings share a common destiny, a destiny that is supernatural. It seems worth the effort to rescue the dogma of original sin from the devastating influence of individualism and to give it its authentic, liberation-oriented content.

What is more, even though the doctrine of original sin does not *directly* obstruct an evolutionary conception of man, it has done so *indirectly* by way of the notion of "polygenism" and it continues to do so today. While polygenism does seem compatible with a "sin of the world," it does not seem to be compatible with "original sin." And since evolutionary thought apparently must accept polygenism, such thought does not seem compatible with the dogma of original sin.

Teilhard de Chardin himself tried to minimize this difficulty,[3] but without great success. And right here we have all the makings of another Galileo case. We find ourselves confronted with a new scientific datum that seems to be directly opposed to a scriptural datum.

This is what Pius XII had to say in his encyclical *Humani generis*: "The magisterium of the Church does not forbid discussion . . . by experts in the human sciences . . . and sacred theology . . . on the doctrine of *evolutionism* . . . But when it comes to that other hypothesis known as *polygenism,* the sons of the Church do not enjoy the same liberty. For the faithful cannot embrace the opinion of those who maintain that after Adam there existed on earth real human beings who did not stem from the first parent of all men by natural procreation, or the opinion of those who maintain that Adam signifies some crowd of first parents. It is in no way evident how this opinion can be reconciled with what the sources of revealed truth and the documents of the church's magisterium propound about original sin" (Denz. 2327–2328).

In other words, evolution itself might be acceptable so long as it is not presented in a mechanistic form, and so long as it did not imply that at some given moment it was not one pair of human beings but whole groups, perhaps separated by great distances, who arrived at a stage that served as the springboard for the slow development and propagation of human characteristics.

For those who accept the hypothesis of polygenism, however, it makes no sense in strictly scientific terms to think that only a single pair was allowed to cross the threshold of humanness and to bequeath this legacy as theirs alone to their descendants. And hence it makes no sense to maintain that this pair alone had the destiny of the species in their hands. It is this viewpoint, grounded in the acceptance of polygenism, that the encyclical has in mind when it says: "It is in no way evident how this opinion can be reconciled with what the sources of revealed truth and the documents of the Church's magisterium propound about original sin."

Three observations can be made about this statement in *Humani generis*. Firstly, as various commentators on the encyclical have pointed out, the magisterium did not affirm that polygenism and the Catholic doctrine of original sin are incompatible. It said that it was *in no way evident* how they could be compatible. One commentator, an insider in the process of working up the encyclical, added that this more prudent way of talking about the incompatibility was motivated precisely by a concern to avoid a new Galileo case. Should theology come to accept polygenism more and more in the future, then the magisterium could say: *"Now it is evident . . ."* Such shadings are important when we know they were an object of express attention.

Secondly, the passage in *Humani generis* indicates quite clearly the specific theological basis for its view that the compatibility of polygenism and the dogma of original sin "is in no way evident." And this theological basis consists in regarding the biblical account of Adam's sin as an *historical* account. But remember that the magisterium now admits that we do not find history, in the classical or modern sense of the word, in the first eleven chapters of Genesis (Denz. 2302). What we find, it says, are the fundamental truths about salvation and a popular description of the origin of the human race and the chosen people—both expressed in simple, figurative terms.

Now if that is the case, then it is clear that all previous declarations referring to "a single sin" and "a single Adam" pick up and propagate this "popular" description of the origin of the human race. Like the apple and the serpent, this unequivocal interpretation cannot be taken *a priori* as a "fundamental truth underlying the economy of salvation." Earlier Councils, the Fathers of the Church, and Saint Paul himself could not speak in a language that did not yet exist but that is ours today: the language of evolution. Hence their reference to an historical sin and an historical Adam[4] cannot be taken to mean that they had formed an opinion about this particular question.[5]

Thirdly, the notion of polygenism itself does not really clash with the classic way of conceiving original sin. It clashes with the classic way of conceiving the *transmission* of original sin. The Christian Church has consistently proclaimed the necessity of baptism,[6] even for those who have not had occasion to commit any personal fault (Denz. 791). This tells us that there is an inborn sin in the human being *as such*. But the way in which the Church has expressed this affirmation, maintaining that this original sin is transmitted "by procreation and not by imitation" (Denz. 790), represents not only a formulated problematic but also a specific response to it.

Our considerations here suggest that it is precisely from a structural perspective on evolution that we can comprehend and appreciate this "sin," which precedes and paves the way for any and every personal *sin* by the mere fact that one belongs to the human species.

II. ORIGINAL SIN AND SEXUALITY

Understandably enough original sin was strongly associated with sexuality in the prevailing Christian mentality, and it continues to be so associated. If our hypothesis is correct, it was not really the biblical account in Genesis that was mainly responsible for this association. Moreover, as we saw, the biblical account of Adam's sin was not interpreted as an account of "original sin" until Paul so interpreted it in his Epistle to the Romans.

However symbolic its presentation may be, the biblical narrative provides little basis for interpreting the forbidden fruit as sexuality. It points out that after their sin Adam and Eve recognized that they were naked (Gen. 3:7 ff.), and that Adam had sexual relations with his wife after the whole drama was over (Gen. 4:1). These details militate against such an interpretation of the forbidden fruit.

Current exegesis, as carried on by biblical experts, is of the opinion that the Yahwist author of this account wanted to portray a case of magic within the context of the idolatry that surrounded the Israelites in his day. The people of Israel were now settled in Palestine, but they were surrounded by other peoples who worshipped fertility gods and goddesses.[7]

Whatever the case may be in that respect, it is our feeling that the reason why popular imagination and literature associate the forbidden fruit with sexuality runs much deeper. We feel that it is deeply rooted in the everyday outlook and living habits of Christianity.

In the context of a Christianity shared by most people, original sin is presented as the event that threw man's life out of whack. Ever since that sin, everything is out of joint. We want to do good, but instead we do evil. Or, as the half-humorous saying goes, everything enjoyable is either forbidden or harmful to our system. And since it seems impossible that this was meant to be the natural order of things, we look to Adam's eating of the forbidden fruit to explain the present condition of man.

Now while we may not consciously advert to the fact, there is no doubt that such structural disequilibrium is nowhere more evident in the life of civilized man than in the realm of sexuality. First of all, we do not have to explore the unconscious with Freud to recognize the extraordinary power of the sexual realm in and on man's life. It is sufficient to realize that sex plays a vital function in defining one's identity for oneself and others and hence in providing self-confidence and security; that it provides the foundation for family life; and that in most cases it signifies a code of iron-clad social laws that have a powerful influence on our friendships, occupations, and living habits. It is only with great difficulty that sublimated forms of sexuality can solve the problems entailed, and this is all the more true in less educated circles.

To take just two factors, consider the great physical and psychic pressure that sexuality exerts directly on the individual and then consider the general situation of most people on a continent such as Latin America. For the vast majority of the people, sexual pleasure is the only pleasure possible for them. It is the only one compatible with their economic status. It is the only one that is cheap enough for people who have been deprived of the economic resources to afford others.

The length of time that lies between the first stirring of sexual impulses in a civilized society and the time when marriage becomes feasible is not a negligible factor either. If the normal frequency of intercourse in marriage suggests a certain biological "normality," then one can get some idea of the problem represented by those long years in which legal and moral impediments are put in the way of what everyone views as the "fulfillment" of man and woman.

Secondly, there is the whole problem of the sexual morality of our "Western" and "Christian" civilization. For our purposes here, it really does not matter whether it is practiced or not. It is enough that it is *the* morality and that it is inculcated as such. Something else would be worth exploring, but it is a very difficult enterprise. We refer to finding out what exactly in this moral code derives directly from the theological elaboration of the Christian message and what stems from the growing repression of any culture that is developing and growing more complex. Freud maintained that such repression and sublimation of the sexual instinct was a precondition for any and all cultural progress.

We do not deny the constant interaction between these two factors. But what interests us here is what is said about sexuality *in the name of Christianity.* And that does not cease to strike us as very odd indeed. In the moral manuals absolutely every kind of sin, except one, varies in seriousness depending on the magnitude of what one does or plans to do. You can kill, but you can also wound someone seriously or slightly, or you can simply refuse to help them. And the gravity of the sin will have a relation to the gravity of the harm done. A lie tht does serious harm is a serious sin; a lie that does not have such serious consequences is a venial sin.[8]

But what happens when we enter the domain of sexual morality? A single slip, in thought alone and independent of any harm to one's neighbor, is grave enough to merit hell with its endless sufferings and eternal separation from God. Pious literature paints numerous examples of spectral apparitions from hell whose sufferings are the result of a single sexual sin which they did not have time to confess or be sorry for.

In our opinion three very serious consequences flow from this widespread outlook and presentation. Here again we shall not try to distinguish between what comes specifically from Christianity, well or poorly interpreted, and what comes from the fabric of a developing civilization.

Firstly, there is no doubt that when sexuality is viewed in this light, it leads morally to a most dangerous moral dissociation. Sex is the wellspring of countless serious sins until suddenly, thanks to some document or matrimonial ceremony, it is transformed into an advisable, holy, and even obligatory thing. But when we consider the power of sexuality, we can clearly see that it must become an integral part of our psychic life before marriage is really possible: "In the first place, it is absolutely essential at that age (i.e., comparatively young people) to integrate sexuality with the whole of the psychic life. When there is stagnation or regression it is often due to an unsatisfactory integration of sexuality." [9]

Now if sexuality is such a pervasive psychic element on the one hand, and we maintain this moral chasm between premarital life and postmarital life on the other, then the only "social" defence against sexuality we can put up is to label it in all sorts of irrational ways. It becomes something "dirty," "impure," "unmentionable," "harmful," and so forth. [10] But how are we going to constructively integrate sexuality into our psychic life if we do that? Sexuality becomes taboo. And this taboo, within the framework of a morality that claims to be rational, either atrophies the whole complex or else is violated.

Contrast this approach with Paul's response to the Corinthians when they queried him about the licitness of extramarital sex relations: "I am free to do anything . . . Yes, but not everything is *for my good*" (1 Cor. 6:12 ff). As we have seen in an earlier volume,[11] Paul is not minimizing the gravity of the matter. He is urging his audience to leave the realm of taboo and to rationally integrate sexuality into a life style that is slowly moving toward complete maturity.

Secondly, the sexual part of what is called Christian morality has a debilitating impact on overall Christian praxis as well. Man's outlook on sexual matters is in large measure a solitary affair, particularly in the light of the surrounding eroticism of society. Now if his eternal destiny is constantly at stake in his attitude toward sexuality, then Christ's single commandment to love one another must drop into the background and suffer severe distortion. The Christian moral life is an eminently social one designed to create solidarity in society. But it is now devalued and turned into an individual struggle to preserve one's chastity. It is as if chastity were something valid for its own sake instead of being meant to serve the social morality of Christianity. Paul's description of this social morality is completely opposed to the morality currently practiced by average Christians: "The person who loves his brother has fulfilled the whole of the law."

Thirdly, it is not just Christian morality that suffers from this terrible, emasculating lack of balance. Faith itself is affected. For centuries the prevailing Christian morality has demanded that Christians regard this earthly life as a *test* in a game plan decreed by God. Quite understandably these Christians came to feel that the logicality or illogicality of the sexual moral code confirmed the fact that the whole business of life was a test and nothing but that. Morality certainly could not be meant to lead people to a progressively more coherent line of moral conduct.

And how were they to picture this "test"? It could only be regarded as the most gratuitously cruel and universally horrifying test imaginable. We must remember that from the Middle Ages on, Christian morality has pictured all men facing the same test. The believer had the rules of the game spelled out for him by divine revelation; the unbeliever learned the same rules from natural law. It is a sociological fact, easily verifiable, that the average Christian puts the same moral gravity on the sexual acts of his nonbelieving fellow citizens—at least on those who share an equivalent degree of civilization.

But how can we possibly picture a good God testing man in this way? How can we believe that he is testing man on some level that is totally independent of his historical and social concerns, which are more universal and more humanizing? How can we believe God is testing man's eternal destiny on the basis of the most despotic and ubiquitous instinctive force of all? How can we believe that the test is based on each and every single act or deed in this sphere, fleeting and private as they may be, rather than on man's gradual effort to dominate and integrate this force into his overall life?

Is it not time to ask to what extent the phenomenon of modern unbelief may be rooted subtly and implicitly in this classic Christian conception of sexual morality and its taboos—which does not seem to be backed up by any portion of the New Testament?[12]

III. WHAT CHRISTIANITY DOES NOT SOLVE

It is our hope that the discussion in the previous CLARIFICATION proves clearly that the Christian message is an overall orientation of one's existence—an orientation that is enriching to the extent it does not claim to possess moral panaceas or a science of behavior that will give one permanent possession of the truth that is necessary to solve moral problems.

The case of sexuality is only one example. Vatican II spoke about the "*numerous* problems which arise in the life of individuals and from social relations" and said that in trying to solve them "Christians are joined with the rest of men in the *search* for truth" (GS 16). Obviously a truth that must be searched for is not one that is already possessed. It is clearly evident that Christianity does not resolve all the problems of history, even though this statement may shock many people. The *theological* fact is that humanity developed for almost a million years before Christianity was provided to it in God's plan. And as we pointed out earlier, this fact can have only one interpretation: Christianity would not have been useful earlier.

It is not easy to explain this long stretch of time from an immobilist standpoint.[13] But it does seem more natural and logical from an evolutionary viewpoint, particularly if we realize that the Christian message enters into a process where progress is the result, not of new injections of energy, but of the redistribution of the invariable energy that was always there.[14]

The fact is that no one claims that the gospel provides solutions for *technical* problems. An engineer must look elsewhere to determine the resistance of various materials. An aborigine must look elsewhere to acquire the dexterity required to overcome the threat of wild beasts.

The problem comes up when people realize that it is wrong to put technical problems and human problems in sharply separated compartments. Our middle-class society is highly specialized and legalistic, and it is the most common source of our concepts. In such a society it is permissible to draw a dividing line, in time and space, between technical efficiency (which provides sustenance) and the human problematic (that is relegated to our spare time).

But the rudimentary findings of anthropology are gradually destroying this compartmentalization. To begin with, there are human beings who are wholly caught up with urgent and peremptory necessities of a "technical" nature. In some cases this is due to the primitive nature of their culture; in other cases it is due to the frequent recurrence of critical situations such as war or a marginal state of living. These people have only enough energy to attend to these urgent needs. Their whole available human effort is concentrated on these needs. Now if one says that the gospel does not provide a response to technical problems, then in such a case only two possible attitudes are left and neither is easy to justify in ecclesiastical circles. On the one hand one rejects the gospel as a dangerous diversion from the task at hand, which requires and serves our whole human effort. Or, on the other hand, Christianity and "technology" are intermingled in such a way that the *rites* appear to be in the practical service of the urgent necessities. In the latter case this comes down to denying in practice what was affirmed theoretically before: i.e., that the gospel, the Christian message, does not provide technical solutions. In that case what are we to say of the gospel? Is it to go on being God's word and revelation? Or is it to become a human technology, necessary or alienating as the case may be?

In the second place, the compartmentalization of technology and human problematic tends to disappear even more when one realizes that relations between human beings are also subject to a "technology." It is distinct from the technology that regulates the relationship between man and things, but it is analogous to this technology. The evolutionary outlook teaches us that societies had to defend themselves against chaos, against anomie (absence of laws), before a profound human problematic could possibly arise. Peter Berger, for example, puts it this way: "Every nomos is an edifice erected in the face of potent and alien forces of chaos. This chaos must be kept at bay at all cost . . . For the moment, suffice it to say that the individual is provided by society with various methods to stave off the night world of anomie and to stay within the safe boundaries of the established nomos." [15]

Berger goes on to add two points of the utmost importance. The first point is that no external control can ensure the cohesion of society. This control must be *internalized*. It is not enough for the individual to consider the fundamental elements of the social order as useful, desirable, and right. Social stability will be ensured far better if the individual regards them as inevitable, as part of the "universal nature of things." [16]

The second point is that this internalization of the law, which is almost always legitimized by the religious realm, begins in a certain way: "To put it a little crudely, legitimation begins with statements as to 'what's what.' Only on this cognitive basis is it possible for the normative propositions to be meaningful." [17] As a result, the individual "*is* whatever society has identified him as by virtue of a cosmic truth, as it were, and his social being becomes rooted in the sacred reality of the universe." [18]

Why do we say that these two points are important for us here? Firstly, because the elements mentioned exist before the gospel and presumably continue to exist as social necessities after it. Even more importantly, however, they are not ignored by the Christian message. Faithful to Jesus' teaching, Paul gives these elements the same name: Greek *nomos*, which means "law." And he declares that the Christian *is not under this law*. Indeed he goes on to say that a person's Christianity is useless and for nought to the extent that he continues to live under the law (cf. Gal. 2:21; 4:11; 5:2; etc.).

We are now freed from the custody of the law because we have reached adulthood. This means we must stop asking "what's what" morally. Instead of asking about the nature of things, we must inquire into their usefulness and benefit to us (cf. 1 Cor. 6:12; 10:23). By very name the Christian is one who does not "internalize" the social order represented by the law; and yet he does not fall into anomie or chaos either (Gal. 5:13).

What is more, the Christian does not accept the "what's what" of the established order. In his process of evaluation the fundamental differences set up by the established order and its "cognitive basis" disappear: "There is no such thing as Jew and Greek, slave and freeman, male and female" (Gal. 3:28).

This lends new and decisive urgency to the problem that one tries to avoid by saying that the gospel does not provide *technical* solutions. On the one hand the survival of any and every society requires that it have mass techniques for internalizing the existing order or the order that is to replace it. Whether it is a matter of conservation or revolution, historical efficacy requires some *law*. On the other hand, the Christian message is by very name the relativization of any such law.

From an evolutionary viewpoint, then, the Christian message must be regarded as *one* moment[19] in the evolutionary dialectic, and not as the totality of the process. To be the total process, Christianity would have to be two things *simultaneously*. On the one hand it would have to be the religious legitimation of the established order, of the law, for the mass majority. On the other hand it would have to be the relativization of this very same law for the creative minority, for those who could prepare a new order and a new law without falling into chaos.

Historical Christianity has in fact often viewed its *universality* as this simultaneous combination of two contradictory things. Now, with the growing trend of secularization, the legitimizing function is being turned over more and more to secular ideologies. People are not asking Christianity to perform this function. They are looking to conservative ideologies (e.g., democratic liberalism) or to revolutionary ideologies (e.g., Marxism) to perform this role.

The latter point will be discussed more thoroughly in later CLARIFICATIONS. What should be clear at this point is that the only universality which the gospel itself proclaims and propounds is the universality of *grace*. And as we pointed out in Volume II (Introduction, Section II), Jesus' use of this word in Luke's Gospel is equivalent to Matthew's use of the word "extraordinary" in the same context (cf. Luke 6:27 ff. and Matt. 5:43 ff.).

The universality of something "extraordinary" does not lie in its becoming a common, ordinary thing. It becomes universal insofar as it fulfills and carries out its extraordinary function, which is nonetheless essential for man's evolution.

IV. *WHAT EVOLUTION CANNOT DO*

Historically speaking, we can say that it was only logical that the rise of the notion of universal evolution would lead to an emphasis on the origin and material basis of those phenomena that seemed to be furthest removed from matter: i.e., those connected with the life of the human spirit.

The lines of thought that followed after the pioneers in various fields were in fact "materialistic," and often called themselves such. This is true of biology after Darwin, psychology after Freud, and sociopolitical thought after Marx.[20]

From what we have already seen in this book, we can readily appreciate the misunderstandings that could result from the use of this term. The most typically spiritual phenomena are indeed the result of a process based on matter, whether we are dealing with the physicochemical plane, the biological plane, the economic plane, or whatever. But this does not mean that these spiritual phenomena do not exist at all, or that they do not constitute a peculiar plane of their own, or that they should not be called spiritual. If someone were to draw such conclusions, he would not simply be invoking the fact of evolution; he would clearly be making an extrapolation on the basis of the *how* of evolution. The fact is that one is or is not a materialist, one does or does not draw these conclusions, depending on how one pictures the process that leads from the most obviously material phenomena to the most obviously spiritual phenomena (e.g., philosophizing or making free choices).

In the next chapter we hope to prove more clearly that any conception of this process that is merely accumulative, mechanistic, and deterministic is in fact identical with materialism. But that is not true of a conception which is truly dialectical, which sees two principles at work from the very beginning and follows the vicissitudes of their opposition and their complementarity.

In view of its importance in the present context of Latin American life, the purpose of this note is simply to devote some attention to Marxist materialism. We want to see to what extent its way of viewing the evolutionary process is materialistic, and we refer here to both the original sources of Marxism and the Soviet version of the theory. Specifically we are going to look at what Marx regarded as the two key moments in the process: the transition from capitalism to socialism (the proletarian revolution and the dictatorship of the proletariat), and the transition from socialism to communism (suppression of the state and of the *a priori* division of labor).

1. The Marxist presupposition that the proletarian revolution is inevitable is not based on any philosophical or religious value judgment on capitalism. Such judgments do exist, particularly in the writings of the young Marx as his use of the notion of alienation would indicate. But basically their only function seems to be to open the eyes of sincere people who are interested in changing things; they do not seem to be meant as an explanation of the world. However, it is not these people who will bring down the capitalist system; the intrinsic economic contradictions of the system itself will do that. The growing impoverishment of the proletariat, which is itself growing because of the industrial revolution, will lead quite naturally to a point where the power of the State will pass from the hands of the few rich people to the many poor people. According to Marx, it will drop like ripe fruit into their hands. Then the proletariat, freely joining together, will make sure that it serves the interests of the majority.

This outlook, perhaps summed up too cursorily here, poses a series of problems that have proved to be acute in later praxis. It would appear, for example, that a key moment in the process of human evolution is here the object of scientific calculation. In the previous CLARIFICATION we saw that Christianity is a summons to liberty, that in its basic principles it does not possess any technique or science as to how to "realize" the content of this summons on the level of human masses. With the Marxist theory, by contrast, we seem to be at the other end of the scale. In principle this could indicate complementarity.

If a decisive event for humanity can be calculated—to the point of knowing what will happen in the capitalist countries that are most advanced technologically—that is so because the behavior of the masses is subject to statistics, and hence to science.[21]

But this brings in another supposition: i.e., that the conduct of the masses is determined more by the calculable features of economic production than by the ideas, values, and legislative measures with which the dominant classes obscure and justify their domination. In other words, the supposition is that the ideological superstructure is determined by the economic infrastructure.

Now the question is: How far do these suppositions go in the thought of Marx? Does the first go so far that it ends up in *determinism*? Does the second go so far that it ends up in what we might call *economism*? If the answer to these questions is "yes," then we could certainly call Marxism a "materialistic" system.

It is obvious that Marx's vision provided the basis for such an interpretation, which was made the official interpretation in the texts of Soviet Marxism. But two important arguments against such an interpretation surface. The first argument is posed by the actual course of events, which gives the lie to calculations formulated in the name of science. Russia was the most backward country of Europe insofar as industrial capitalism was concerned. Yet the first socialist revolution took root there, thanks to a careful analysis of the superstructure. On the other hand human ingenuity mitigated the internal contradictions of industrial capitalism to such an extent that Marx, writing to Engels in 1858, talked about the "bourgeoisification" of the English proletariat brought about by the rise in their standard of living.[22]

Both facts give the lie to any "science" of man, even one based on mass lines of conduct and economical determinants. And they also force one to give more and more importance to the "party" of the proletariat: that is, to the conscious vanguard that will raise the consciousness of the rest of the proletariat. And here Lenin enters the picture: "And indeed, Lenin's strategy of the revolutionary avant garde pointed to a conception of the proletariat which went far beyond a mere reformulation of the classical Marxian concept; his struggle against 'economism' and the doctrine of spontaneous mass action, his dictum that class consciousness has to be brought upon the proletariat 'from without' anticipate the later factual transformation of the proletariat from the subject to an object of the revolutionary process."[23] There is no doubt that Lenin's pamphlet entitled *What Is To Be Done?*, in which these ideas find their classic formulation, was written in the context of the internal struggle between Russian Marxists to take control of the backward proletariat and assume leadership over them. But their implications extend far beyond this context.[24]

To begin with, they eliminate any interpretation of Marx in terms of mechanical economism and foster a dialectical interpretation. But they do more:

> The trend of large sections of organized labor toward "class coopera-
> tion" . . . threatened to vitiate the notion of the proletariat as the revolutio-
> nary subject on which the whole Marxist strategy depended. Lenin's formu-
> lations intended to save Marxian orthodoxy from the reformist onslaught,
> but they soon became part of a conception that no longer assumed the
> historical coincidence between the proletariat and progress which

the notion of the "labor aristocracy" still retained. The groundwork was laid for the development of the Leninist party where the true interest and the true consciousness of the proletariat were lodged in a group different from the majority of the proletariat. . . . Lenin's strategy of the avant garde acknowledged in fact what it denied in theory, namely, that a fundamental change had occurred in the objective and subjective conditions for the revolution." [25]

In other words, the complexity of revolutionary praxis had to recognize the "human" complexity of mass conduct. If a "science" was still required, it could not be one based on mere "mechanical calculation" or "economic determinism." This science of man would have to take into account another factor and treat it as decisive. And this factor was the ideological superstructure that explains and determines the behavior of both the conservative and the revolutionary minorities.

This practical discovery leads to another discovery in the realm of theory. It seems that the original Marxism foresaw the simplistic interpretation mentioned above and ruled it out from the start. Engels explained the view shared by both him and Marx this way:

> Production is the determinant factor, but only '*in the last instance*'. '*More than this neither Marx nor I have ever asserted*.' Anyone who '*twists this*' so that it says that the economic factor is the only determinant factor, '*transforms that proposition into a meaningless, abstract, empty phrase*.' And as explanation: "The economic situation is the basis, but the various elements of the superstructure—the political forms of the class struggle and its results, to wit, constitutions established by the victorious class after a successful battle, etc., juridical forms, and then even the reflexes of these actual struggles in the brains of the participants, political, juristic, philosophical theories, religious views and their further development into systems of dogmas—also exercise their influence upon the course of the historical struggles, and in many cases preponderate in determining their form."[26]

Thus if we are going to take seriously the lessons of reality *and* Marx's system itself, we must fully accept the dialectical nature of evolution and take into account the decisive importance of a factor that is essentially "nonscientific" in *the first instance*: i.e., the ideological factor.[27]

> We must carry this through to its conclusion and say that this overdetermination does not just refer to apparently unique and aberrant historical situations (Germany, for example), but, is *universal*; the economic dialectic is never active *in the pure state*; in History, these instances, the superstructure, etc.—are never seen to step respectfully aside when their work is done; or, when the time comes, as his pure phenomena, to scatter before His Majesty the Economy as he strides along the royal road of the Dialectic. From the first moment to the last, the lonely hour of the "last instance" never comes.[28]

2 Now if evolution never gives us the transition from capitalism to socialism all wrapped up neatly in a package, then the transition from socialism to communism is an even more uncertain thing. And we are talking about communism as Marx pictures it: i.e., the transition to a

society without classes or differences, without an imposed division of labor, and without any need for the control and repression ordinarily exercised by the State.

Marx thought that the socialist revolution would take place in those capitalist countries that were most technologically advanced. And he also thought that the transition from the socialist stage to the communist stage would be a quick one. One would not have to contend with the exacerbation caused by artificially induced needs, and one would have the productive capacity of an advanced technology at one's disposal. Thus one could envision that in a short time everyone would have what they needed without a great expenditure of effort. In such a situation the division of labor would not be based on scarcity or the profit motive; it would be based on the vocation of each person. Since there would be no need for compelling people to do disagreeable work, the State and its repressive force would be unnecessary and superfluous. The picture of this future society is described vividly in a famous passage of *The German Ideology*.[29]

In a very interesting study Franz Hinkelammert shows that this seemingly scientific image is in fact a *limit concept*: i.e., an ideal that society can only approach negatively by eliminating the obstacles that turn the division of labor into a mechanistic and oppressive factor. The assumption is that by eliminating these obstacles we can get rid of repression completely and make social necessities and the division of labor coincide with the vocation and satisfaction of each and every individual. But that is asking evolution to do something which it itself cannot accomplish. Ignoring the specifically human plane, we are asking evolution to accomplish the leap to the borderline-limit.

At this point we might do well to consider two passages in Soviet literature of the Stalinist era. The first is a bold affirmation of utopia. The second expresses doubts about the possibility of achieving this utopia scientifically. Both passages come from the writings of Leonid Leonov (b. 1899). The first passage comes from his novel entitled *Road to the Ocean*:[30] "A mass of sparkling, humming insects were whirring melodiously in the air around me. I imagined that they too were singing . . . I watched one of them that had separated from the rest. It crashed at full speed into a lamp post and fell to the ground, its wings folded contentedly in death. That is how the problem of death was solved there."

The second passage comes from *The Kormilitsin Case*.[31] Two characters are talking about the new society that will come:

> "The new man will create new human beings in his own image and likeness. In other words, he will be a god. He will be the soul of the gigantic machinery that will provide a plentiful supply of food, clothing, and pleasure."

"That is interesting," agreed Kormilitsin. "I have always enjoyed reading about the *miracles* of science and technology. But what about *the people* themselves?"

They will have different associations . . .For example, you might have an association of southern or northeastern linen producers. The only government organ would be the central office of planetary statistics that would make up annual comparative charts."

"And who would draw conclusions from these charts?"

"Well . . .Marx said nothing about that. But that is only a minor detail."

"Wait, I am talking about the man in whose hands all the threads of perfect knowledge will gather. Now don't get angry with me, but what if this man is an *egotist* like you, Protoklitov?"

"Such a man would be incapable of doing any damage. What is more, he will be superior . . . "

"But can you recall any deity of the past who did not have defects?"

Protoklitov began to get angry . . . He never liked provincial bumpkins.

That is what evolution cannot accomplish for us. And what was voiced as a doubt in Leonov's story is affirmed outright in other Marxist texts that probe more deeply. Consider this statement by Milán Machovec: "Once the more complicated social problems are solved, we will be left with this vast movement molded by an atheistic tradition . . . However difficult the task may be, it will be forced to explore all existing human dimensions and all conceivable human dimensions. Radically abandoning God, Marxism will sooner or later be forced to pick up the heritage of the 'human mystery.' " [32]

NOTES

1. Piet Schoonenberg, *Man and Sin: A Theological View*, Eng. trans. by Joseph Donceel (Notre Dame: University of Notre Dame Press, 1965), pp. 177 ff.

2. Remember what we said earlier: the Genesis account of Adam's sin became a teaching about original sin only after Paul's commentary on it!

3. According to him, science cannot determine how the mutation was achieved which serves as the starting point for what we call the human species. It seems to be a biological law that the more critical mutations are, the more imperceptible they are. And the more imperceptible they are, the less traces they leave. As Teilhard de Chardin sees it, it is perfectly possible that the passage to the human level was effected by a single pair, which was able to transmit this basis to various and different human families or "phyla." We then would have *monophyletism*, which is all that is required by the terms and context of *Humani generis*. See Teilhard de Chardin, *The Phenomenon of Man*, Eng. trans. by Bernard Wall (New York: Harper & Row, 1957), concluding pages of Book III, Chapter I.

4. Particularly the latter, because as we saw earlier the word *Adam* is a

collective noun meaning "man," not a proper name as it is today. See Schoonenberg, *op. cit.*, pp. 126–131.

5. This is in line with a general principle accepted by all theologians. It says that when we are examining statements of the magisterium and biblical passages, we cannot look to them for answers to questions that the authors of these documents did not ask themselves.

6. Or of the equivalent grace that non-Christians receive without the sacramental sign of it (GS 22).

7. See Gustave Lambert, "Le Drame du Jardin d'Eden," in *Nouvelle Revue Théologique,* 76 (1954), pp. 917–948, 1044–1072. The tree of 'the knowledge of good and evil' seems to be the tree that promised man knowledge of everything in the practical order. The serpent would be the image of various divine entities who promised their devotees fertile soil and fruitful wombs.

8. We should note the relationship between the notion of the harm done to one's neighbor and the one *Christian* commandment (John 13:34; Rom. 13:8–19; and so forth). Even though this is formally noted in the manuals, it shows up in connection with all the commandments relating to our neighbor except those dealing with sex. In sexual matters, for some unknown reason, the harm done to one's neighbor does not affect the gravity of the sin or even determine its essential nature. Consider Paul's line of argument against the use of prostitution, remembering that he gives a social and existential sense (not a sexual sense) to the word *flesh* (1 Cor. 6:15,18; see also 1 Thess. 4:3–8).

9. Raymond Hostie, *Religion and the Psychology of Jung,* Eng. trans. by G. R. Lamb (New York: Sheed and Ward, 1957), p. 47.

10. Don't forget that for centuries Christianity had to combat tendencies that saw every exercise of sex, even within marriage, as something evil (Denz. 430).

11. See Volume I, Chapter V.

12. Interestingly enough, if one takes a quick glance at the New Testament Gospels to find a sin that is condemned in even its minor manifestations, he will find that the sin in question has nothing to do with sex but with neighborly relations: "Anyone who nurses anger against his brother must be brought to judgment. If he abuses his brother he must answer for it to the court; if he sneers at him he will have to answer for it in the fires of hell" (Matt. 5:22). An exegesis of the "blasphemy against the Holy Spirit" in proper context indicates that it has to do with refusing to share in Jesus' liberative task. No serious exegete would equate it with any sexual sin.

13. The argument that this length of time was required for the proper preparation of the Israelite people is not very convincing. Jesus' message breaks with Israelite tradition to such an extent that the majority of them reject it. On the other hand the pagan world, without any preparation, opens up to the new revelation, as Paul and Acts indicate.

14. Grace, a supernatural energy, is not a "new" energy in the sense that it breaks through at some specific point in time. See Volume II, Chapter III, CLARIFICATION II.

15. Peter L. Berger, *The Sacred Canopy* (New York: Doubleday & Company, 1967), p. 24.

16. *Ibid.*

17. *Ibid.*, p. 30.

18. *Ibid.,* p. 37.

19. "Moment" in the functional sense rather than the temporal sense. A function can be permanent and still have its own specific and critical efficacy in a process: its moment.

20. To what extent the creators themselves were materialist is difficult to determine. As often happens, they themselves may have been more taken up with their important discoveries and been little concerned with this question.

21. See Chapter II, CLARIFICATION II.

22. Letter of October 7, 1858.

23. Herbert Marcuse, *Soviet Marxism* (New York: Columbia University Press, 1958), p. 31.

24. Both in the countries where the proletariat was "backward" and in those where it was "immature" or "bourgeoisified."

25. Marcuse, *Soviet Marxism, op. cit.*, pp. 31–32.

26. Letter to Bloch of September 21, 1890. Cited by Louis Althusser, *For Marx*, Eng. trans. by Ben Brewster (New York: Vintage Books, 1969), pp. 111–112.

27. Earlier we pointed out that Christianity does not and cannot provide a science or technology of mass lines of conduct. Here we must stress the fact that Christianity cannot refuse to analyze the "ideological" elements bound up with its theology, which is elaborated by the ruling classes.

28. Louis Althusser, *For Marx, op. cit.*, p. 113. According to Althusser, it is this that may qualify Marxism to judge situations that were not foreseen by Marx himself. In this book, he cites the case of Latin America as one such situation.

29. "Finally the division of labor offers us the first example of how man's own actions operate against him so long as he lives in a natural society. In such a society a division exists between particular, individual interests and the common interest. Activities are not divided up on the basis of man's voluntary will but on some natural basis. Man's own actions are turned into an alien and hostile force working against him. Instead of man dominating his acts, they dominate him. As soon as a division of labor starts, each individual moves in a specific, closed circle of activities which is imposed on him and from which he cannot escape. He becomes a hunter, or fisher, or shepherd, or deprived of the basic necessities of life. In the communist society, by contrast, the individual is not bounded by a closed circle of activities. He can develop his capabilites in the field that appears best to him. Society is entrusted with the task of regulating the general production. So it becomes quite possible for me to do one thing one day and another thing another day. I may fish in the morning, hunt in the afternoon, and play the critic in the evening. I do not have to be a hunter, or fisher, or critic exclusively" (Karl Marx, *Die deutsche Ideologie*, in *Werke*, Berlin: Dietz Verlag, 1962, Vol. 3, p. 33.

30. Original title, *Doroga na Okean* (1935).

31. Original title not verified.

32. Milán Machovec, *Lettre* (May 1969), p. 30.

CHAPTER FIVE

The Human Evolution of Sin

In the preceding chapters we have verified the fact that sin, far from disappearing, takes on truly cosmic dimensions in an evolutionary conception of the universe—just as it does in divine revelation. So one might well be inclined to ask why the evolutionary outlook has been accused of ignoring sin.

As we intimated at the outset of this volume, this accusation is not without solid foundation. The mental mechanism that makes an authentically evolutionary view of the universe possible is the use of analogy. Therein lies its strength and its weakness.

Thanks to analogy we can compare different phenomena and regard them as steps in the same process. For example, we can relate the complex psychology of a mammal to that of an echinoderm; or we can relate the complex calculations used to study the reactions of a living cell to those which must be used in studying the behavior of a basic molecule in a piece of rock.

The fascination that the evolutionary process has for the human mind lies in the fact that one can bring together various processes, compare them, and interpret them as parts of one whole: e.g., the oxidation of a metal, the heliotropism of a plant, the reflexes of an animal, and the mental operations of a human being. Undoubtedly the fascination is due in large measure to the fact that only this joint comparison enables man basically to free himself from the compartmentalization of the universe and to embark on the adventure of coming to know the whole.

Section I

Perhaps the most interesting and important thing here is to distinguish two different ways of conceiving the whole, two different ways of comparing the bits of data that come from different scientific fields. Both ways may be labelled "evolutionary" in approach, but in fact only one of them really merits that label.

The first approach is not really based on an *analogy* between the processes that take place at different levels of the universe. It is based strictly on what is common to all of them. However advanced and complex the processes may be, the fact is that they all have the same physico-chemical base we find in lifeless matter. The procedures that are serviceable in studying the latter can—and should—be transferred to all the phenomena of the universe without any retouching or analogy being employed. On this level comparison points up progressive differences which, up to a certain point, can give rise to a real evolutionary conception.

In physical terms, for example, one can compute the *per capita* increase in energy available to humanity from the remote past to the present day. Comparative study of these computations will reveal a "quantitative" evolution toward more *per capita* energy, thanks to the use of domesticated animals, steam power, electricity, and atomic energy.

The disadvantage of this first way of conceiving and studying evolution certainly does not lie in the inexactness of the computations—as if the mental processes of the more civilized human being introduced new energy magnitudes from another direction. The difficulty lies in the fact that as the study of basic levels (e.g., the physico-chemical level) is applied to higher levels, it proves to be more and more incapable of helping us to understand the phenomena that are peculiar to the new, higher levels. The increase of energy signified by the shift from electric energy to atomic energy is a fact, an important fact. But in itself it does not suffice to explain the cultural phenomena that arise when human beings divided by physical and ideological frontiers find themselves for the first time faced with the possibility of destroying a considerable portion of the human species.

We certainly cannot construct a "political science" by disregarding or overlooking the data that come from the physico-chemical ground level, because the latter continues to be the ground of political phenomena. But probably no one would claim that political science is—or can be—a mere extension of the methods applicable in physics or chemistry.

In spite of the perdurance of phenomena of the same order at every level of the universe, what Teilhard de Chardin says in one of his letters is true: "The mystery of every circle of the world lies in *the next circle*." [1]

Now however much of an evolutionist a man of science may be, the fact is that the various scientific specialties, each with its own methodology and language, are distinguished from one another by the "static" cross section they carve out for themselves in reality. They logically have a tendency to apply their specialty, with its language and methodology, to other levels; that in itself is justifiable. But they also are logically inclined to give way to routine in making this application and to ignore the "mystery" of the new level, which may require different procedures to handle it adequately.[2]

Thus the process of making our knowledge universal is effected by a procedure which may indeed penetrate everything but which becomes further and further removed from the global phenomena among which man must decide in order to give direction to his history.

The human mind moves toward the second way of conceiving evolution when it begins to suspect, through the use of analogy, that the complex processes observed in man are related to, and even directly descended from, other simpler processes observable in the origin of life and even in the inner organization of inert matter.

For example, the notion of *facility*, of the easy or convenient way out, is familiar to us in psychological and political processes. And using analogy we can transfer this notion to other levels of the universe.

The realm of culture shows us that man's bold conquests have been followed by a process of mechanization, quantification, and uniformalization. This process actually reintroduces many of the defects of prior situations because it operates in terms of the easier way. That is what happened to the ideal of "liberty, equality, and fraternity" espoused by the French Revolution. That is what happened to socialism when confronted with the alienation generated by capitalism.

Doesn't this fact have some relation to the fact that entire species of animals have disappeared because of the *facility* they gained from some particular attribute? Some particular attribute made things easy for them. So they developed it quantitatively, uniformly, and mechanically until what had been an advantage reintroduced a fragility presumably excluded by it.

And do we not find *facility* operative at an even more elemental stage? Does it not dominate the arrangement of inorganic matter on the physico-chemical level, making it highly improbable that complex life-producing syntheses will take place? Does it not account for the fact that life is a fragile and infinitesimal portion of existing matter, however decisive it may be?

Now in the three examples we have mentioned, the term *facility* is analogous. When one is talking scientifically, it will be replaced in each of the appropriate disciplines by concepts that are more precise and operational. Even more importantly, these concepts will differ in accordance with the instruments that each discipline operates with.

Yet we would maintain that in this analogy lies our hope for a truly evolutionary and truly operative knowledge of the universe. And we would say that it does not lie in any simplistic reduction of the whole universe to one single basic language—that of physics, or chemistry, or mathematics, or logistics. The reduction of the whole universe to the most basic phenomena gives rise to a purportedly evolutionary conception that ignores guilt, conflict, dialectics, and ultimately redemption as well. It unjustifiably transfers the certitudes of the preceding circle to the "mystery" of the following circle. For example, when it is considering the realm of liberty—that is, the sphere where evolution is in the hands of man—it carries over into this sphere the determinisms that ruled evolution when control over it was more external to the individual and when adaptations to problems of the milieu were effected in a mechanical or almost mechanical way.

Only a "reductive" conception of evolution can ignore sin and redemption. An "analogic" conception cannot. Only a "reductive" conception can give the impression that an evolutionary view of the universe entails denying the unknown factor of human liberty in favor of some obligatory and necessary line of progress that runs counter to the data of both concrete experience and theology—not to mention the political dimension of history.

But the fact that the indeterminacies of the lower levels are transformed into freely made decisions when the threshold of the human level is passed cannot blind us to the fact that determinisms continue to be operative on the human level.[3] Human liberty cannot excise these determinisms. Instead it must take them as the foundation for its freely made decisions.

And that leads us to take one step further. Starting from this richer notion of evolution, we shall try to move further in our attempt to link up the concepts of evolution and guilt.

Section II

There does exist an "analogy" that runs through the whole process of universal evolution. It is almost too obvious, being little more than a quantitative consequence of the principle of entropy: every rich synthesis is difficult, improbable, and a seemingly fragile minority affair vis-à-vis less rich and more facile syntheses.

The amount of hominized energy is infinitesimal by comparison with the energy deployed in the totality of vital phenomena. And life in turn is quantitatively little more than a negligible minority by comparison with the quantity of inorganic matter.

Let us consider a midway term: life, organic matter that is vegetable or animal. Wherein lies the support for its existence, continuity, and preservation? Paradoxically enough, it lies in the circles that precede it and that follow it. It lies in the majority quantum of inorganic matter and the minority quantum of thinking matter.

We have already pointed out that despite the resistance that facile syntheses offer, it is their multitude that makes possible the difficult and the improbable. Life would not have arisen without the "facility" with which matter falls back into simple syntheses and infinite repetitions. It is there that chance can operate with a certain "liberty" and now and then indulge in the luxury of more complex and difficult syntheses. An example from a different field may help us to understand this better. The primitive tribes that still exist today do not open themselves to a more complex and fruitful civilization precisely because the separation into small tribes does not give chance enough numerical possibilities to produce renovative personalities. Mathematically speaking, we can say that such people have arisen when large human conglomerates have formed numerically suitable fields for the rise of critical, renovative minorities—however much hidebound and resistant to change the components of these conglomerates may have been.

But life is in turn defended from its great numerical weakness by minorities that are even smaller than it. As we noted, thinking matter is an infinitesimal minority within the totality of vital energy. And yet it is man who guarantees the reign of life in the universe by developing life's fertility and fecundity, selecting more resistant animal and vegetable species, and establishing links between organic matter and the inorganic matter that is more capable of nourishing and developing the qualities of life. And who but man explores inert matter and finds in it new sources of energy that seem to suspend its descent to utter coldness indefinitely?

Thus the consistency of the universe seems to depend on the convergence of two dialectically opposed forces. One is physical entropy at its most evident stage. The other is love and liberty at the level where its dimensions are most obviously perceptible. And each can be found in some less obvious form where the other seems to be more obvious. At the level where entropy dominates the scene we find chance, indeterminacy, and the interplay of possibilities as the almost imperceptible germ of what will later be liberty and love. At the level where love clusters all the energies of the universe for their maximum potentialities we find entropy, almost imperceptible, taking the form of sin, that is, the easy road of egotism and routine that leads to disintegration.

One thing should be stressed in this connection. An analogic conception of evolution is based on a recognition of these two dialectical forces there *where each one of them is most clearly evident*. Viewed from this vantage point these forces would bear the names "entropy" and "love" respectively. But the evolutionary outlook consists in recognizing that both forces are present and active in different ways in all the stages. In the realm of the physico-chemical, love is *chance*, indeterminacy. In the realm of human mental processes, entropy is *sin*.

This explains why a conception that is evolutionary only in a "reductive" sense has projected on to the human realm perspectives that are simultaneously *individualistic* and *gregarious*, where only chance breaks the determinist line of sure and steady progress. Despite Marx's efforts to assimilate it into his thought, the fact is that the historically reductive evolutionism of the nineteenth and early twentieth century served as an ideological basis for justifying capitalistic competition.[4]

Despite the partial truth it contained, the "natural selection" of Darwinism represented a "reduction." It pictured the more developed stages as a throw-back to more primitive stages. Hence it failed to explain and generate more solidary societies. And that also explains the improvisational approach used by official Marxism in constructing socialism. Being "reductive" by virtue of its mechanistic materialism,[5] it had to *improvise* the motivational links between the initiative of the individual and the common task; and there were many failures and setbacks along the way. In this context a work like Ernesto (Che) Guevara's *El socialismo y el hombre en Cuba* ("Socialism and Man in Cuba") is flagrant heterodoxy vis-à-vis the official materialism of Marxism. At the same time it represents one of the most fruitful ways of linking up the problems of present-day society with the living thought of Marx. And it also represents a reformulation of the major questions of Marxism in an evolutionary context that is analogic rather than reductive, and that is therefore much more fruitful and human.

If someone acknowledges the viability of a society that does not seek to be based on material stimuli, if someone believes that at this stage of human development man is capable of devoting his interest to the solidary evolution of mankind, then is he not in fact attributing central value to redemption and sin even though he is talking in terms of economic and political categories and even though he may not mention these words?

Why do we find this constant attraction being exerted by the higher levels of evolution when the only fixed and calculable feature is the consistency of the lower levels? Whence comes this *chancy* but indestructible victory over entropy? Whence comes this ever more manifest attraction exerted by the future instead of the past, in a evolutionary process that began with what was clearly a majority tendency toward regression?

The fact is clear enough. The proper interpretation of it is not. The Christian sees it as a continuing work of "redemption" from entropy, which is at first imperceptible but then grows more and more evident. At the human level it is "redemption" from sin, which is the form that entropy takes there. This redemptive force is love, the life of God becoming more and more present in the universe until it becomes a human being like any other human being in history.

In a mysterious way this sheds light on one of the greatest enigmas in the New Testament. In an earlier volume[6] we alluded to the curious nature of the process described in the Prologue to John's Gospel. The Word draws progressively closer to the final stage in which he comes "to dwell among us" (John 1:14). As this process comes to a head, rejection becomes quantitatively more noticeable and significant. Fewer and fewer people attend the approach of the Word. Christ, made man among men, gives his few followers the power "to become children of God" (John 1:13). In this small nucleus of people, the process of hominization is confronted with its loftiest evolutionary possibilities. At this point we might be inclined to say what one commentator on Teilhard de Chardin said: "What matters the rarity of living substance if its quality reaches such a height?" [7] But that is not the way Teilhard de Chardin or John's Gospel looks at the matter.

The Prologue to John's Gospel tells us that the Word returns to his Father after he has given this potentiality to his followers. But he does not return surrounded only by this small nucleus whose quality has reached "such a height." He bears with him the total whole that seemed to have been spurned by virtue of its refusal to penetrate and explore this new quality. How could that have been possible? In the same way that it is possible in the overall process of evolution. The seemingly fragile and tenuous layer of hominized matter is the element that supports and renews and liberates all of nature that did not reach that stage. The "quality of such a height" that Rideau mentions, the "full extent of his love" of which John the Evangelist speaks (John 13:1), do not find their explanation or terminus in themselves. They constitute the most potent force for transforming everything else.

Section III

Thus, starting out from a conception of evolution we feel is right, sin and redemption take on their most universal and decisive significance and converge to establish the principal lines of a Christian morality.[8]

1. A moral doctrine that proceeds from divine revelation is also a

moral doctrine that takes due account of what has been revealed: i.e., God's plan for the universe. And this plan is strictly social. Nor does evolution lead to any other destiny. The only destiny that still retains the character of a goal for humanity, the one that is supremely analogous to all the thresholds already passed, is the goal of a society in which each individual person directs his creative potentialities toward the common good. And we must not forget that the very solidity and consistency of the lower levels and of the entire universe depends on the higher-level syntheses. *Everything*, in the strictest and most absolute sense of the word, depends on whether or not we do approach such a society. On that depends the survival of humanity and the potential concentrations of physical energy in the universe.

Besides not being evangelical, individualistic morality has been superseded by political events and telluric happenings. It belongs to the era when the lower circles were evolving by natural selection. At that point they were fighting each other for the right to survive and thus serve as the launching pad for new possibilites.[9] But at the stage we are now: "The egocentric ideal of a future reserved for those who have managed to attain egoistically the extremity of 'everyone for himself' is false and against nature. No element could move and grow except with and by all the others with itself . . . The outcome of the world, the gates of the future, the entry into the super-human—these are not thrown open to a few of the privileged nor to one chosen people to the exclusion of all others. They will open only to an advance of *all together*" [10]

Hence the politicizing of morality is not a escapist approach. The discovery of the inescapably political interpretation of the gospel is the logical and fruitful end result of a humanity that has become conscious of humanity as a universal phenomenon and accepts the challenge of heading it toward the future.

The politicizing of morality is escapist when it is "reduced" to solutions of a mechanical, mass-level sort. It is escapist, in other words, when social syntheses reproduce the poverty, uniformity, and forced synchronization evident in the component elements—either through the direct use of force or through the indirect force entailed in a competetive process that leaves the individual no alternative.

2. We said that love is the *final* goal of this social morality because the society based on it, unlike the one we have just described, shows up as a "*synthesis of centres.*" [11]

A society comes to be based more and more on love to the extent that it refuses to reduce its members to quantitative uniformity, to the extent it is structured in such a way that each one of its elements may contribute the totality of his or her creative power to the whole. What love effects

on the interpersonal level or the level of small communities is thus transformed into a goal for human societies taken individually and as a whole.

But in this evolutionary perspective love is not a predetermined
norm. As we have already seen, it is a vector that traverses the whole
evolutionary process in very different and graded ways. The gratuitous
and efficacious way in which it manifests itself to us in the Gospels is
merely one of its forms, one that is conditioned by the end results of
evolution as a whole.[12]

Various forms of egotism—or if you prefer, of love bound up with
egotism or natural selection—have been positive vectors at other stages.
And there is no reason to assume that these stages no longer exist in any
human situation.[13] No present-day society—not to mention any society
of the past—has been able to leave the free expression of personal
creativity entirely to the individual human being. With its impersonality
law is a form of violence, of selection, of organized egotism; but at the
same time it is the necessary base for any and all progress.

By the same token a law that discriminates between the members of a
given society on the basis of race or social class or private property is a
brake impeding progress to another stage when the possibilities of
reaching that stage are there. And this latter stage is one where the law,
again with its dose of impersonal violence, is in the service of a greater
solidarity. It would be unrealistic and certainly un-Christian to invoke
gratuitous love when only a certain "class egotism" or "race egotism" can
serve as the springboard toward new and greater solidarity.[14]

Invoking these same qualifications and reservations, we can say that
"violence is not Christian." In the last analysis violence is a simplistic
form of social synthesis that fits in with primitive situations. But such
situations can be maintained and even re-created by man's poor han-
dling of evolution.[15] To say that violence does not construct anything
durable is a monumental historical error—as is the notion that violence
suffices to solve human problems at every stage.

3. On the basis of the features we have highlighted so far, we can
now understand something that may seem quite surprising to us: the
moral attitudes which Jesus himself stressed as proper correlates of his
message are not classified as "obligatory" by Christian moralists.

The more sketchy formulation in Luke's Gospel (6:27–35) may not
bring out the force of the passage as clearly as Matthew's parallel presentation does (5:21 ff.). In the latter Jesus constrasts *his own* law with the
tenets of the ancient divine law: "You have learned . . . But what I tell
you is this" (cf. Matt. 5:22, 28, 32, 34, 39, 44).

What does come through clearly in Luke's gospel is the *unity* of Jesus'
exigencies. The "old" law stressed things that man was generally inclined

to do anyway: love those who loved him, help those who helped him, lend things on the assumption that they will be returned, etc. Jesus' law is one that talks about deeds based on gratuitous giving, on *grace* (Luke 6:32–34).

Now attitudes centered around "gratuitous" giving are not escapist, are not insensitive to love's need to be efficacious, so long as they are not taken to be *legal* exigencies. Blessing those who curse us, offering the other cheek to someone who hits us on one cheek, giving our coat to the man who takes our shirt, and lending to people who cannot repay us —all these things are examples, and only examples, of an adventure in gratuitous giving with which the whole doctrine of the gospel is bound up.

These dicta were not existing laws. They pointed toward a love that was efficacious in its very gratuitousness. Jesus was the first to regard them, not as a static norm (cf. Luke 6:29 and John 18:22–23) but as the goal of a creative effort which is sensitive to those moments in the life of a group or a society when only this gratuitousness is capable of new and richer syntheses.

We are people who "have come to know and believe the love which God has for us" (1 John 4:16). With his death and resurrection Jesus proved to us the radical and thoroughgoing efficacy of gratuitousness.

The fact is that only an evolutionary outlook on sin and grace, entropy and love, violence and gratuitous giving, can hope to be in line with the message of the gospel.

And we would offer one final observation. This adventure in gratuitous living, this pageant of redemptive grace opposing sin, is essentially a minority affair—as is life, as is man, as is the play of ideas.

In Luke's version the gospel poses this question: "If you love only those who love you, what credit [i.e., grace] is that to you?" (Luke 6:32). In Matthew's gospel it is put a bit differently: "If you greet only your brothers, what is there *extraordinary* about that?" (Matt. 5:47; our italics). Matthew underlines the extaordinary nature of the thing that is being asked of us. And it is extraordinary, not so much because few people value such attitudes, but because the triumph of love throughout the evolutionary process is never a quantitative one. It is a minority affair without being an elitist one. It is a minority affair because it wells up from the entropy-ridden base that continues to dominate quantitatively even on the human level. It is not elitist because the love which thus comes to life is at the service of negentropy in the universe. It structures the universe for syntheses that are richer, more human, more redemptive.

NOTES TO CHAPTER FIVE

1. November 20, 1918. Cited by Emile Rideau, *The Thought of Teilhard de Chardin*, Eng. trans. by René Hague (New York: Harper and Row, 1967), p. 434.

2. Hence "scientists" are not "evolutionists" to the extent they think they are. But some are: those whose "cross section" is in itself dynamic, such as geologists and paleontologists.

3. See Volume II, Chapter IV, CLARIFICATION II.

4. To take one Latin American example, here is what one writer has to say about the conservatism of Martínez, a Uruguayan politician and statesman: "It is worth noting the *doctrinal roots* of his conservatism . . . His individualistic posture was bound up with *the principles of social Darwinism that were systematized by Spencer*. It was bound up with the idea of selection through competition within the industrial society that had succeeded the military society. This conservative ideology, carried from the institutional order to the socio-economic regime, can be separated from the evolutionist philosophy taken in itself, although he did not do this" (Arturo Ardao, *Etapas de la Inteligencia Uruguaya*, Montevideo: Dept. Publicaciones Universidad, 1971, pp. 172–173).

5. Perhaps very different from the "realistic" materialism of Marx himself, or at least of an important version of his thought. See Chapter IV, CLARIFICATION IV.

6. See Volume III, p. 110.

7. Rideau, *The Thought of Teilhard de Chardin, op. cit.*, p. 78.

8. Complementing those indicated in Volume I, Chapter V.

9. "Life advances by mass effects, by dint of multitudes flung into action without apparent plan. Milliards of germs and millions of adults jostling, shoving and devouring one another, fight for elbow room and for the best and largest living space. Despite all the waste and the ferocity, all the mystery and scandal it involves, there is, as we must be fair and admit, a great deal of biological efficiency in the *struggle for life* . . . 'Survival of the fittest by natural selection' is not a meaningless expression, provided it is not taken to imply either a final ideal or a final explanation" (Teilhard de Chardin, *The Phenomenon of Man*, Eng. trans. by Bernard Wall, New York: Harper and Row, 1959, p. 109). As this natural selection leaves the conduct of evolution in the hands of its own protagonists, it is as if its finality were turned upside down: nothing can evolve further without causing the whole to evolve too.

10. *Ibid.*, pp. 244–245.

11. *Ibid.*, p. 294.

12. See Volume III, Chapter IV, CLARIFICATION I.

13. If we take seriously the notion that *solutions* are not prepackaged for us in advance (GS 16), then the dictum that violence is not Christian holds true for violence as an ideal, not for violence as a possible solution.

14. The same thing occurs on the psychic plane, which reproduces the process of evolution in the species and the universe. Analogy is again operative. See the texts of Freud (*Civilization and Its Discontents*) cited in Chapter I, CLARIFICATION I.

15. For example, the institutionalized violence denounced by the Medellín Conference.

CLARIFICATIONS

I. TOWARD AN EVOLUTIONARY PASTORAL EFFORT

We do not see why the Church's pastoral effort, its activity as a community in the midst of mankind, should shun or be exempt from an evolutionary orientation that holds true in all the other sectors of existence. Vatican II points out that the Church "goes forward together with humanity and *experiences the same earthly lot which the world does*" (GS 40; our italics). What is more, "the pilgrim Church in her sacraments and institutions, which pertain to this present time, takes on the appearance of this *passing* world" (LG 48; our italics). As the context of the latter passage clearly indicates, the reference to the "passing" nature of the world and hence of the Church does not refer to its frailty or future disappearance. Rather, it situates the Church alongside all the creatures that wait, groaning in expectation, for their recapitulation in Christ at the climax of salvation history.

Hence, as we have already remarked,[1] it would be an error to turn Christian pastoral activity into an a-temporal activity impervious to the vicissitudes of history, to construe it as some sort of locus of eternity in the midst of time.

Because of divine revelation Christian pastoral activity cannot ignore evolution. Evolution is a reality, a theological reality, that must take place on both the ontogenetic and the phylogenetic level—i.e., in each individual and in humanity as a whole. Saint Paul talks about unfolding Christ's teaching for his hearers according to their degree of maturity (1 Cor. 3:1–2; Heb. 5:12–14). And the whole history of humanity proves that the gospel was deemed useful and advantageous to man only after a long period of human preparation for it. The Old Testament is one brief, localized stage of the overall process. The ten centuries that went into its actual redaction are nothing compared to the thousands of centuries of human prehistory that went before it.

But even that is not enough. Pastoral activity is a creative activity. It is not enough to prove that such an evolution did take place and is still going on, even in the area of relations between God and man. To paraphrase one commentator on Teilhard de Chardin, it is not simply that reality is in a process of evolution. Our way of thinking about things, once confronted with this fact, must become evolutionary as well.[2] In other words our thinking, which will give orientation and direction to our praxis, must take on a certain cast; we must start to think, evaluate, and plan in evolutionary terms.[3]

1. Thus there is no question here of establishing the best possible pastoral approach—not even for "the present moment." "*The* present moment" does not exist. Nor did the right moment exist for *the whole universe* to receive the message of the Old Testament. God's "pastoral activity" in the Old Testament era found its moment not only in time but specifically in the concrete dispositions of the Aramaean tribes living in Palestine under a monarchy about a thousand years before Christ. And the New Testament did not dovetail with "the right moment" for humanity either. Aside from its initial roots in Judaism, it coincided with "the right moment" for only one specific sector of humanity: that portion of humanity living under Roman rule in the Mediterranean basin.

The denial of *one* universal "present moment" for pastoral activity has critical importance for the Church's presence in the "Third World," i.e., in those countries which stand on the periphery of the great economic empires. Hence it is critically important for the Church's presence in a "Christian" continent such as Latin America.

Pastoral activity, like any activity that is conscious of its evolutionary base and framework, must adopt as its basic criterion the simple and obvious dictum formulated by Teilhard de Chardin: "Nothing is constructed except at the price of an equivalent destruction." [4] The word *equivalent* may be ill chosen, since it suggests that the thing destroyed was of "equal value." But if it were of equal value, the whole significance of evolution would be eliminated. What Teilhard de Chardin really means is that every "construction" is a displacement, a new distribution, of the energy that remains basically constant. Older possibilites are disenfranchised in favor of other possibilities conceived to be of greater value. What is clearly impossible is the maintenance of both simultaneously.[5]

Pastoral activity, then, cannot consider what it gives (and what it demands) as something purely positive. Even when it is a question of the most lofty mystical values, more "lowly" possibilities and capabilities are annulled. And we never know in advance or *a priori* whether it is beneficial to pay this price.

Seen in this light, Medellín's document on peace does not issue a summons to the Church and its pastoral activity to take on an additional duty. What it proclaims is part of the basic criterion for judging the usefulness of any sort of pastoral activity. It says this, for example: "As the Christian believes in the productiveness of peace in order to achieve justice, he also believes that justice is a prerequisite for peace. He recognizes that in many instances Latin America finds itself faced with a situation of injustice that can be called *institutionalized violence*

... violating fundamental rights. This situation demands *all-embracing, courageous, urgent,* and profoundly renovating transformations ... One should not abuse the patience of a people that for years has borne a situation that would not be acceptable to anyone with any degree of awareness of human rights" (n. 16, our italics; MED II, 78). Now every pastoral effort displaces energies. And every pastoral effort in Latin America, which is affected by the situation just described, displaces energies in the face of an "institutionalized violence" and the need for "all-embracing, courageous, urgent, and profoundly renovating trans-formations." Is it too much to ask that our pastoral activity calculate, as scientifically as possible,[6] the impact of this displacement of energy on the concrete needs posed by the existing situation?

2. We face diverse situations with different "energy" demands —both material and spiritual. But in practice the Church, confronted with these different situations, carries out its pastoral activity with an unchanging body of truths, sacraments, and canonical laws. The under-lying presupposition is that a person is or is not a Christian. And if one is not a Christian, pastoral practice comes down to making sure that this person becomes a Christian or returns to the fold he has left.

But a truly evolutionary pastoral effort is a realistic effort that takes account of man's concrete needs. On the basis of these needs it builds what Paul pointedly called the *oikonomia* ("economy") of the mysteries of God (cf. 1 Cor. 4:1; Eph. 1:9–10; Eph. 3:2–3). Such a pastoral effort cannot make out Christianity to be this unvarying, undifferentiated block.

What is more, we live on what is called a "Christian" continent. It is a continent that is somehow related to the religious message of Christ. Hence to some it seems that we cannot recover the freedom which God, the revealer and teacher *par excellence*, displayed in his dealings with the people of Israel. How, for example, can we return to the "distribution of energy" that followed from the belief that Yahweh was *exclusively* the God of Israel and transfer this utter trust and simplicity to those who must fight desperately for a measure of justice that will permit them to be human in a basic way? Some argue that we have gone beyond that stage, thanks to the gospel and its universalism, and it would be an *error* to go back.

Our feeling is that the use of the term *error* in this context is akin to calling a mother a liar when she tells her children the story of Little Red Riding Hood even though she herself does not believe it. The gospel itself shows us that Christ's disciples went through different stages of the Old Testament outlook before arriving at truths they could bear (cf. John 16:12). And even after Pentecost they were not what we today could unreservedly call "Christians."

If the Church gave up its focus on the anonymous multitude,[7] if it lived on its own resources attentive to the real needs of Latin Americans, it would be much more "pluralistic" in Paul's sense of the term (Rom.

14:1 ff). It would pay much more attention to the pre-Christian stages of faith,[8] i.e., to the necessity of seeing the Old Testament as much more than a religion that has now been superseded and is therefore false. Instead it would look to the Old Testament for phases of a revelation adapted to historical situations—situations that have not disappeared with the passage of time, situations that are reproduced "ontogenetically" and "phylogenetically" (i.e., in the life of each individual and periodically in humanity as a whole during the course of history.

II. IS THERE A CHRISTIAN MORALITY FOR EVERY AGE?

If we must accept an evolutionary conception of the whole universe, then the Christian message itself must be inserted into this process. Far from relativizing the message, this insertion markedly enchances its import. Earlier in this series we suggested that the originality of this message had to remain relatively latent until man discovered that he was simultaneously the product of past evolution and the one responsible for universal evolution in the future.[9] To take one example, we could not fully grasp and appreciate a creative, progressive morality—one that dovetailed with man as a mature child of God—until we had undertaken the task of desacralizing the world and dominating it by technology.

Thus the Christian message could be conceived as the revelation of what we are and must do, a revelation made at one point but covering every stage equally. The final judgment of humanity presented by Matthew's Gospel (Matt. 25:31 ff) applies equally to Neanderthal man and to twentieth-century man. The measuring rod is real, effective love, described by Matthew in terms of its content closest to home: food for the hungry, water for the thirsty, and so forth.

Now if the Christian message referred solely to this, it would be nothing more nor less than the historical mentality breaking through at a given point in time but capable of being applied to any stage of evolution. This would have a great advantage. But the fact is that evolution is not uniform. Even though today we cannot actually witness the transition from the quadrumana to man anywhere we can observe extremely primitive human situations. These situations, due to stagnation or regression, are situations in which love must be particularistic, exclusivistic, violent, and solidly based on instinct if it is to be efficacious.

From the evolutionary viewpoint we can simplify the panorama by citing these observations of Will and Ariel Durant:

> Moral codes differ because they adjust themselves to historical and environmental conditions. If we divide economic history into three stages —hunting, agriculture, industry—we may expect that the moral code of one stage will be changed in the next. In the hunting stage a man had to be ready to chase and fight and kill. When he had caught his prey he ate to the cubic capacity of his stomach, being uncertain when he might eat again; uncertainty is the mother of greed, as cruelty is the memory—if only in the blood—of a time when the test of survival (as now between States) was the

ability to kill. Presumably the death rate in men—so often risking their lives in the hunt—was higher than in women; some men had to take several women, and every man was expected to help women to frequent pregnancy. Pugnacity, brutality, greed, and sexual readiness were advantages in the struggle for existence. Probably every vice was once a virtue—i.e., a quality making for the survival of the individual, the family, or the group.[10]

We cannot minimize, for example, the "moral" impact of such a fundamental cultural change as that embodied in the transition from hunting to agriculture: "We may reasonably assume that the new regime demanded new virtues, and changed some old virtues into vices. Industriousness became more vital than bravery, regularity and thrift more profitable than violence, peace more victorious than war.[11]

We can readily appreciate the fact that in both situations or stages just described it is *objective* love that must and will be the criterion of judgment proclaimed by the gospel. But Jesus goes even further to bring the point home to the person who has no memory of these situations, to remind him that it is not some a-temporal absolute that will be used to judge what it good or bad about his conduct. Jesus challenges the morality that the Old Testament derived from God himself and hence absolutized: "Nothing that goes from outside into a man can defile him . . . It is what comes out of a man that defiles him" (Mark 7:18,20). Mark is the only evangelist to advert to the concrete impact of this relativization on the moral conscience of the Christian community: "Thus he declared all foods clean" (Mark 7:19–20). There was reason to emphasize this point at the time, considering its importance for Judaism. But Jesus' words go much further: "It is what comes out of a man that defiles him. For from inside, out of a man's heart, come evil thoughts, acts of fornication, of theft, murder, adultery, ruthless greed and malice; fraud, indecency, envy, slander, arrogance, and folly" (Mark 7:20–22). Jesus' principle revolutionizes *the whole* of morality: things do not come into the sphere of human activity already bearing the moral label of "good" or "bad." Ethical value adheres to the whole project within which they are inscribed as means and tools.

Jesus' principle embodies the morality that can cover all the stages of human evolution. If someone should ask whether violent tactics and armed resistance are compatible with Christian morality, we can frame a reply by paraphrasing Jesus' statement of the principle: "It is not what comes to man from outside that is immoral, but what comes from inside a man. From the heart of man comes true evil—with or without arms —and from the heart of man comes true hunger for justice—with or without arms."

That is the Christian message, the only one that is compatible with a humanity involved in a process of evolution. But is that the only Christian message? Luke filters out some of Matthew's adventitious remarks and presents in summary form the demands of Jesus that go beyond those of the Old Law: "But to you who hear me I say: Love your enemies; do good to those who hate you . . . When a man hits you on the cheek, offer him the other cheek too; when a man takes your coat, let him have your shirt as well . . . When a man takes what is yours, do not demand it back" (Luke 6:27 ff.).

Once again we would seem to be confronted with a morality that is established for man before it has been inscribed in his plans and purposeful actions. It seems to be a morality that comes to him from outside rather than coming from inside him. But if we are going to be logical and consistent here, we must say that this is not the case, that it cannot be the case. It is not a morality of a-temporal, moral precepts. *Efficacious* love is the only demand imposed by Jesus for all time.

But in the passage just cited and in many others, Jesus calls our attention to another kind of *efficaciousness* that is possible for love. It is a form of efficaciousness we tend to spurn in our normal everyday lives: *the risky adventure of gratuitousness*, of grace-full living.

Thus when we look at a concrete historical reality, such as our own situation in Latin America today, we can interpret the gospel in one of three ways:

1. The first interpretation ignores evolution and identifies "gratuitousness," "nonviolence" *à outrance* with the gospel message. For postevangelical epochs the most efficacious love is the kind recommended countless times by Jesus: i.e., not resisting evil with evil.

2. The second interpretation accepts the fact that the gospel certainly does propound a "gratuitous" love. But it reminds us that this characteristic is *subordinated* to another characteristic of decisive importance: the need for love to be *efficacious*. Thus we must "de-situate" the gospel, stripping from it what the Christian community added[12] to it on the basis of its own situation. We must get down to the substantive message of Jesus, which is not bound to any particular time: all men will be judged by the efficacity of their real-life love.[13]

3. The third interpretation tries to maintain both the tension and the unity of the first two interpretations. The gospel does tell us that efficacious love is the only criterion of divine judgment. But the gospel also presents this panorama of gratuitousness, without indicating in detail how, when, and to what extent we ought to exercise it. And it presents this notion of gratuitousness so that its enunciation of efficacious love being the only criterion will be something more than a tautology, something more than a mere confirmation of the fact that sincere human beings have always done good. The revelation that God is love is meant to open up new vistas of efficaciousness.

Why do we say that there is tension in the third interpretation? Because adopting this outlook is not simply equivalent to taking note of these

evangelical propositions. It is the task of a whole lifetime in which we try
to imprint the "reflexes" of gratuitousness on our way of life. If this is
not done in a serious way, then our attempts to mimic these propositions
will be mere caricatures. "Turning the other cheek," for example, will be
an artifical action that will be a mere parody of what efficacious love
should be.

Now at this deep level any and every transformation psychically
structures the whole person. Here is an example. A scientist might recognize that in certain situations it would be more useful or even absolutely necessary for him to act with the instinctive caution of a primitive
Indian. He may recognize this, but he cannot do that. In terms of the
real-life demands he faces, he is suffering from "professional malforma-
tion," however important that formation may be within the overall social complex of today.

Realizing this, let us take a look at our three interpretations insofar as
they generate typical stances in the Catholics of Latin America.

The first stance rejects the use of certain methods (e.g., violence) as
being anti-evangelical, no matter what the human situation may be. It
turns "gratuitousness" into an absolute, nontemporal precept of Christianity.

The second stance accepts the efficaciousness of love as the one and
only criterion. In situations of violent injustice,[14] it feels that the only
thing the Christian should be worried about is the possibility of love
being ineffective.

The third stance is more complex. In theory it accepts the formulation of those who adopt the second stance. But it brings in the example
of the trained scientist to explicate its full position. Just as you cannot
expect the trained scientist to display instinctive intuitions and attitudes,
so you cannot expect the Christian—who has determined to make his
whole life an adventure in gratuitousness—to plunge into the dynamic
of an instinctive struggle where love can turn into an "instrument for
killing" for the sake of being efficacious. Thus this stance accepts the fact
that real love functions in this atmosphere; but it also notes the psychic
impossibility of fully participating in this efficacy. There we have the
Christian tension that can truly be present in the real-life situations
which our continent is presently experiencing.

Over against this tension will be situated the tension that tends to
sacrifice everything to immediate efficaciousness. Any other kind of
efficacy of a more long-range sort will be ruled out. If this tension is
truly lived and overcome, then Christians who are deeply Christian will
shoulder the task of efficacious love when new conditions decide the
issue: i.e., whether the stimulus for active solidarity should be physical,
economic, or moral.

III. THE VIOLENCE OF OMISSION

It has been said that the greatest sin we Latin American Christians
commit is the sin of *omission*. And the paradox is that it does not seem to

bother us. So true is this that it was deemed advisable to change the
Confiteor of the Mass a bit, replacing "through my fault" with a reference to "what I have done" and "what I have failed to do."

We have already pointed out that every sin is essentially antihistorical. To say no to God is to say no to a God who is known and reached in
and through history. To deny God, in other words, is to deny him in his
revelation. It is to deny the man Jesus who has a plan for the universe:
with the collaboration of his fellow men he plans to gradually lead the
universe toward its recapitulation, toward its full and complete meaning.

Now the present-day Christian frequently tends, if not to "recapitulate," at least to "sum up"[15] his moral conduct in terms of the one and
only commandment: Love one another as I have loved you. But this kind
of summary of the commandments does not rid them of their traditional
cast as prohibitions. In other words, the commandment to love others is
summed up in the prohibition not "to harm" our neighbor.

In such a summary the *creative* obligation of love is mutilated terribly.
Why? Because the most efficacious love is not a love that avoids occasions
of harming others; it is a love that moves evolution forward and leads it
toward more human forms and structures of life.[16]

For example, the occasion to kill or not to kill another person will
rarely present itself to us in our lifetime. But in fact international wars
daily occasion the death of hundreds and thousands of human beings.
The commandment, "Thou shalt not kill," leaves us feeling perfectly at
ease because none of us in Latin America is directly *killing* anyone in
Vietnam. And that is why some Christians feel that participation in a
public anti-war demonstration is a *merely political* gesture. To put it
another way, these Christians would be greatly shaken if they were suddenly confronted with the option of killing another human being, but
they do not feel a bit shaken when they are presented with the *positive*
possibility of forming a powerful international movement against a war
in which thousands of human beings are being killed. Looking out a
window at a passing demonstration against the war in Vietnam, it would
never occur to them that they are failing, by omission, to comply with the
commandment not to kill insofar as it is a component of the one and only
Christian commandment: that our love be efficacious.

Every Latin American can undoubtedly cite examples that are closer
to home. And this omission takes on even greater importance and deci-
siveness when we advert to the dialectical rhythm of evolution.

As we indicated earlier, a complex and fragile rhythm is operative
between majorities and minorities, between sin on the structural level
and love on the interpersonal level, between adaptation on the one hand
and criticism on the other hand. It is not a question of two things being
absolutely contradictory.

Now every new sociopolitical endeavor, every opportunity to structure society in a better way, must entail at some point a rapid adaptation
of people's conduct. In other words, it does not leave room for the

critical sense and the inner conviction of each and every individual. To take two examples at the opposite ends of the scale, this was true of the bourgeois revolution and it was also true of the proletarian revolution. (The terms are admittedly far from being exact.)

In these circumstances, the minorities may look upon the use of mass-oriented processes for the implementation and solidification of the new order as sin. Omission shows up here in an elitist outlook that applies one's own moral principles to condemn the management of crowds and multitudes. One removes himself from this "sin" and disowns it at the very moment that the process of evolution demands it and redeems it. Omission here takes the form of utopian withdrawal and isolation, which is closely bound up with passive criticism and passive opposition.

But passive adaptation to the new order must be wary of sinning by omission too. Once this new order has been legitimized and legalized, once it has been translated rightly or wrongly into morality, passive adaptation sins by omission every time it rejects new and revolutionary possibilities that promise to be even more fruitful. It sins by omission when it does not heed the creative criticism and heroism of new minorities, when it spurns the "sin" of dangerous, dissonant conduct.

In both cases morality evolves, yes, but against the current of authentic evolution. It becomes a useless weight instead of serving as a force that will guide us into the future.

Here omission reveals its underlying nature: it is not dialectical. Positive morality is not creative by virtue of the "will power" with which one says no to temptations. It is creative insofar as it is sensitive to *the critical moments* in the life of the individual and of society. For it is at these critical moments that a thrust which was once sound and constructive can turn into something directly opposite if it is extended too far, if its functionality is stretched beyond its real worth.

Thus the greatest activist can commit the sin of omission. For the morality that guides evolution has two poles, and a creative rhythm runs between them. God works *with* the sin of human beings—not just *in spite* of it. Human beings cannot fall back on a greater purity than that.

NOTES

1. See the CLARIFICATION in Chapter I of this volume.
2. See Madeleine Bathélemy-Madaule, *Bergson et Teilhard de Chardin* (Paris: Ed. du Seuil, 1963), p. 43. Our mind and spirit, still attached to the "supernatural," does not pay heed to evolution. Teilhard de Chardin makes a pointed observation: "A long animal heredity might well have formed our limbs, but our mind was always above the play of which it kept the score. However materialistic

they might be, it did not occur to the first evolutionists that their scientific intelligence had anything to do in itself with evolution" (Teilhard de Chardin, *The Phenomenon of Man*, Eng. trans. by Bernard Wall, New York: Harper and Row, 1959, p. 220).

3. This does not mean terms that are *relativistic*. It does mean terms that are *relative*, in the sense that all reality must be put "in relation" to man in accordance with objective laws. Why does something that is common practice in pedagogy seem shocking when it is applied to the Christian message, its truth, and its relationship with praxis?

4. *The Phenomenon of Man, op. cit.,* p. 51.

5. On the basis of his continuing clinical practice, Freud concluded that the *premature* formation of moral reactions was to be counted among the factors predisposing a person to a later neurosis.

6. One can at least say that this does not seem to be a major preoccupation of "religious sociology."

7. See our book, *Acción Pastoral Latinoamericana: Sus motivos ocultos*, soon to be published by Búsqueda of Buenos Aires.

8. See our book, *Qué es un cristiano* (Montevideo: Mosca, 1971), Part I, "Las etapas precristianas de la fe."

9. See the magnificent passage in which Teilhard de Chardin describes this decisive step: "Hitherto men have been living at once dispersed and closed in on themselves, like passengers who have met by chance in the hold of a ship without the least idea of its mobile nature or of the fact that it is moving. Living, therefore, on the earth that grouped them together, they could think of nothing better to do than quarrel among themselves or try to amuse themselves. And now, by chance, or rather by the normal effect of the passage of time, our eyes have just been opened. The boldest of us have made their way to the deck, and seen the ship that carried us. They have noted the creaming of the bow-waves. They have realized that there are boilers to be fed and a wheel to be manned. Above all, they have seen the clouds above them and smelt the fragrance of the islands over the circle of the horizon. The picture of men ceaselessly in agitation over the same spot has gone; this is no longer an aimless drifting, it is a *passage to be made good*. It is inevitable that some *other* sort of Mankind must emerge from that vision" (*La montée de l'autre*, 1942, in *L'activation de l'énergie*, cited by Rideau, *The Thought of Teilhard de Chardin*, Eng. trans. by René Hague, New York: Harper and Rown, 1967, p. 302).

10. Will and Ariel Durant, *The Lessons of History* (New York: Simon and Schuster, 1968), pp. 37–38.

11. *Ibid.*

12. When Christians must work in collaboration with persons or groups who hold different ideologies, they are often greatly concerned about their own identity as Christians and try to figure this out before committing themselves to active effort. They want to know what is their "specific contribution" *as Christians*. It should be noted that in Latin America today there is a tendency to regard this question as a poorly framed one. On various occasions Hugo Assmann has expressed this opinion, his view being in line with the second stance outlined in this CLARIFICATION. Here is what he says on one occasion: "Pardon me if I emphasize what might seem obvious. Christian revolutionaries do not constitute any 'historical subject' that can be specified in terms of being Christians ... This does not at all rule out the validity of the term 'Christian

contribution.' What it does is get beyond the traditional way of formulating and posing this question. That formulation conceived the 'Christian contribution' as some specific thing, alienating and serving as a brake of some sort. It was pictured as some sort of doctrinal *a priori* that took precedence over revolutionary process. This sort of notion was dangerously and idealistically opposed to the inevitable mediation of united praxis in the unique revolutionary process and it was the classic source . . . of the 'third way' approaches that could be manipulated by the forces of reaction" (Hugo Assmann, "Prologue" to *Habla Fidel Castro sobre los cristianos revolucionarios*, Montevideo: Tierra Nueva, 1972, pp. 22–24).

13. The "gratuitousness" of love is often recognized to be an ideological element which, by comparison with other methods, redounds to the advantage and maintenance of the status quo. Thus the suspicion of ideological interpretation, which seems quite logical when applied to historical theology, penetrates as far as the sacred writings themselves. Since the latter are already an interpretation, why should they be free of "ideology"?

14. Or of "institutionalized violence," as Medellín puts it.

15. When Paul declares that all the ancient precepts are now "recapitulated" in the precept of love (Rom. 13:9), the original Greek word means much more than a summing up. To *recapitulate* things is to frame things in such a way that they acquire their full meaning. This does not mean that the precepts are forgotten or broken down without recapitulation. It simply means they lack their "head" and have no moral import.

16. Vatican II is aware of this danger and adverts to it with very clear examples: "Profound and rapid changes make it particularly urgent that no one, ignoring the trend of events or drugged by laziness, content himself with a merely individualistic morality. It grows increasingly true that the obligations of justice and love are fulfilled only if each person, contributing to the common good, according to his own abilities and the needs of others, also promotes and assists the public and private institutions dedicated to bettering the conditions of human life. Yet there are those who, while professing grand and rather noble sentiments, nevertheless in reality live always as if they cared nothing for the needs of society. Many in various places even make light of social laws and precepts, and do not hesitate to resort to various frauds and deceptions in avoiding just taxes or other debts to society. Others think little of certain norms of social life, for example those designed for the protection of health, or laws establishing speed limits. They do not even advert to the fact that by such indifference they imperil their own life and that of others" (GS 30).

Conclusions·

1. From Christian revelation we know that a divine force carries individual human beings, the human race, and the whole universe toward their recapitulation in Christ. "Recapitulation" here does not mean a mere summing up. It means that each and every element of human history and the universe is united with its head: i.e., with its deepest inner meaning. Every person and every thing acquires its authentic, definitive signification therein.

We know that this cosmic force is love (GS 38). It is the life of God himself given as a present to man. Thus it is the gift par excellence: *grace*.

There is no doubt that the term *grace* , unlike the word *love*, has been used *ad nauseam* in theology and Christian catechesis—to the point where it has become a depersonalized and reified notion. On the other hand the term *love* can lead us astray too, not because of the ambiguous lines of conduct it may suggest but precisely because it points us toward an interpersonal relationship primarily. Because it does this, it can lead us to forget the social character of God's gift on the human plane and its universal character on the cosmic plane. In reality God's gift starts all earthly dynamisms on the road toward complete hominization—that latter being a gradual transition from compulsion to freely undertaken action, from coercion to grace.

Understood in this sense love, grace, life, and God's gift make up the positive vector of evolution. On the human level it is recognized as such through faith. But in infinitely less perfect and perceptible forms it is present in every aspect of the cosmic process.

On the other side of the coin, deliberate opposition to God's grace has always been called "sin"; and its ultimate motivating force, which leads to the denial and rejection of love, has been called egotism. But here again, as we have tried to point out, the classic Christian outlook is in for a suprise when it looks at the New Testament. The earliest thinkers in the New Testament did not set up an opposition between Jesus on the one hand and the sin of one person against another person on the other hand. Nor did they focus on egotism, which causes the failure in authentic interpersonal relationships. As they saw it, Jesus' enemy was a force as great as the universe itself. Jesus does battle against a sin which is much more structural than that resulting from the deliberate, cold-blooded decision of an individual human being. Using terms like *world* and *flesh*, the New Testament writers also suggest that sin, the opponent of hominization, has more primitive forms at every level of the universe.

Understood in this sense egotism, sin, and enslavement to the world and the flesh make up the negative vector of evolution. This is the obstacle that evolution must overcome so that what is new and positive can make its way to its complete fulfillment: i.e., to its recapitulation in Christ. All sin is anti-evolutionary; and in its less conscious and perceptible forms its restraining influence pervades the whole cosmic process.

2. Now if love does constitute the positive vector of evolution, this is due to the fact that its very essence is to unite *different* beings without blotting out their differences. We can translate this point into terms that apply to the whole evolutionary process. When any given problem calls for a response or a solution, the response or solution can come about in one of two ways. It can be brought about by a facile solution that reduces the differences involved. Or it can be brought about by a much more difficult synthesis that effects unity but leaves open the different possibilities of each element. We end up with a synthesis of centers instead of a mere aggregate. As such, love can be defined as the guiding norm of the universal process.

On the other side of the coin, sin shows up as a satanic decision to invert the whole process. The sin with which the New Testament is familiar is not barefaced egotism. It is that brand of egotism which does indeed look for solutions but which is unwilling to pay the price for better solutions. The richer, less immediate synthesis is sacrificed in favor of more immediate, impoverished syntheses. The instrinsic wickedness in this surrender to the easy way out lies in the fact that this approach ignores the differences of other beings: i.e., their character as centers. Facile syntheses—sin—reduce other beings to the common denominator of their short-term usefulness. Oversimplification and the recourse to facile, immediate solutions are the perduring features of those lines of conduct which put a brake on evolution each time it seems possible to look farther ahead and accept greater complexity.

3. If we add the quantitative factor to the preceding, we find that the facile syntheses are translated into statistical majorities at every level of evolution and on every plane of human existence. They make up the

majorities that are subject to laws—these laws being more or less precise depending on the level at which the different sciences work.

We see indeterminacy already operative on the simplest levels of the physico-chemical world. Little by little it is transformed into a capacity to escape the rule of statistical laws, to shoulder a destiny with a mediate and complex view of the means that will lead to it. But escape from the law, that is, escape by the difficult road, makes love the minority *par excellence*. In each and every being love, the law of all evolutionary progress, is that which has been withdrawn from the realm of the mechanical, the habitual, the probable. It is *liberty* vis-à-vis a sin, the latter always being a relapse into what is quantitatively the majority.

What we have just discussed is something that is becoming more and more *visible* on the plane of social conduct—due to such phenomena as the worldwide growth of urbanization, industrial production, and mass communications. The whole theme of *masses* and *minorities* (or elite groups) grows increasingly relevant.

But the door is left open to a great deal of ambiguity here, however little the terms may be confused on the linguistic level. What is *merely* quantitative does not determine quality, even though the latter is translated into quantitative terms through the mechanism we have examined earlier. Thus, for example, the mere accumulation of power, prestige, or money in the hands of a given individual or group does not make this individual or group a minority (in our sense) vis-a-vis the great number of people who have been dispossessed of these same goods. Even though sociology often operates with these terms on the quantitative level and defines "masses" and "minorities" accordingly, these two terms have a deeper and more fluid import here.

Take the case of someone who "creates" a great deal of monetary wealth. He belongs to a "minority" insofar as this term means control over complex economic mechanisms and long-range planning. But this very quest for wealth can be directed by motivational forces that are as base and simplistic and immediate as those of the people whose poverty helps to make him rich. From our point of view the "mass" here would include both the rich exploiter and the majority of the exploited; the "minority" would be those who use money solely as a means, a very ambiguous means, of serving the common good.

We could give many more examples because the same basic structure shows up on many different planes. We find it in the realms of power, prestige, love, education, consumption, and so forth. *Masses and minorites do not exist in any absolute sense.* What we find are mass and minority patterns of conduct on *each and every level of life.* Someone can be part of the minority on one level and part of the mass on another level. And he will have to be that on other levels, as we shall see.

4. So far we have been talking about positive and negative vectors of evolution in rather watertight compartments: love versus egotism, grace versus sin, difficult syntheses versus facile syntheses, liberty versus law, minority lines of conduct versus majority lines of conduct. One term in each pair represents the driving force behind evolution, as it were, while the other term represents a brake on evolution. Now we must confess that our division is far too simplistic.

Evolution is not a contest between two contradictory forces that would cancel each other out, unless one should partially or totally eliminate the other. Though they point in opposite directions, these two vectors—or tendencies, or forces—are indispensable and complementary, *each in its own way*.

We stress the last phrase because the quantitative majorities impose conditions on the qualitative minorities *in spite of themselves*. The mass element ignores the minority element. It deprecates and oppresses the minority element even though it is the precondition for the latter's potential work. In turn authentic minorities—i.e., ones that are not merely elitist behavior patterns based on every man for himself—*are cognizant of* their conditioning by the mass and *are deeply concerned* about elevating it on a mass level. At the same time they are concerned about salvaging from the mass all minority lines of conduct that are possible and useful. In other words, they do two things: (1) they stir up and promote the whole spirit of criticism—not that which is purely destructive but that which is concerned about mediate and complex syntheses; (2) they mechanize (i.e., inject the easy facility of the purely mechanical into) lines of conduct that are more complex and results that are more mediate.

That is how evolution has proceeded, analogously, from the very beginning—though our formulation here is based on the plane of human intentions.

5. Sticking here to the human level, we see that every social system functions, or is created, through an interaction between masses and minorities. To avoid possible misunderstandings already noted, we can make this more specific: every social system functions, or is created, through an interaction between mass sociopolitical lines of conduct and minority sociopolitical lines of conduct. In other words, minority and mass factors must be at work whether the aims envisioned are conservative or revolutionary.

Contrary to what people often think, revolution is born not of chaos but of order. Order, based on mass lines of conduct, must provide the base for a creative minority. From this base the minority, capable of conceiving a more complex and potentially richer social order, arises and acquires effective size. If this new order crystallizes, however, then it must immediately generate mass lines of conduct that will guarantee a stable foundation.

In other words, social evolution—and we do not use that term here as the opposite of revolution—has *two critical points.* If these two points are not noted and respected, they will inject a radical change of direction in the preceding movement. If on the one hand the elaboration of mass behavior patterns reaches the point where it stifles the growth of critical minorities (facile synthesis), then the purported protection of society turns into the direct opposite. If on the other hand the critical minorites do not seek out mass processes for implementing their goals, if they remain enclosed in revolutionary ghettos populated by those who share the same ideas (again, facile synthesis), then in fact they destroy the effectiveness of their own criticism and are absorbed into the prevailing system. Again we get a complete reversal of direction.

So we see that there is a mechanism, a *dialectical* rhythm, at work in the interaction between masses and minorities, facile syntheses and difficult syntheses, sin and grace. We readily admit it is not easy to explain what we mean by "dialectical" here. The word is very much in fashion but it is also extremely vague.

Here we do not intend to give it the meaning that classical Hegelianism or Marxism gave to it. Nor do we intend to decide whether the original thought of Hegel or Marx presents a richer and more complex conception of dialectics than the classical conception did. That is not part of our purpose here.

Let us just say that the evolutionary process is not dialectical in the sense that the contradiction or tension between the two opposing terms is the origin or mainspring of movement. Cosmic energy, like human energy on its own proper level, would move just as much without the positive vector. But it would move inexorably in the direction indicated by entropy: toward a process of continuing degradation. Nor does the "positive" vector enter into the process fraught with a messianism such as that which devolves on the proletariat in Marx's dialectic.

We use the term *dialectic* here only because it seems indispensable in trying to define the following fact: if either of the two vectors or tendencies interacting in evolution steps beyond a critical point in relation to the other, then it turns around and operates in the opposite sense. For that very reason this dialectic pervading history must be turned into a theological key to understanding the life of Christ. It is an indispensable key to any and every Christology.

6. As we have seen, only a dialectic of this sort fits in with the totality of the Christian message. When Christ bade us to love one another as he had loved us, when he gave us that one commandment, he was not presuming to rectify the mechanism of evolution and humanization. He did not bid us to exercise a celestial, disembodied love that would be ineffective and even harmful. He did not set up his Church as a community "alongside" the human community, as a parallel community dispensed from the latter's concern to move evolution forward and to arrive at the creation of a more human society.

To transpose the notions of grace and sin, love and egotism, outside the coordinates of efficaciousness governing history is tantamount to denying the gospel. But one can also deny the gospel by failing to recognize where the proper function of the Church lies. While the gospel does accept *the whole dialectical process*, it expects the Christian community to perform a function that is equivalent to *one of the two poles*: the minority.

Only from this vantage point can we appreciate why Christianity applies the word *sin* to all mass lines of conduct even though it realizes that they are and always will be necessary. Only from this vantage point can we understand its deep-rooted emphasis on gratuitousness as an "efficacious" venture in love. Only from this vantage point can we see why it opposes the "world" and the "flesh" as dynamisms that drown out criticism and liberty.

In the overall dialectical process, a mass Christianity would represent a denial and negation of the tension. A minority Christianity on the other hand signifies, or should signify, a formidable dialectical thrust within the whole process. For this to happen, two factors must be combined. A recognition of the *global* process must be combined with a conscious awareness of its own *particular* and specific place in this process. That is the vocation and the tension weighing on every Christian and on the Church's pastoral activity. If the Church does not have a correct understanding of the relationship between evolution and guilt, it will not be able to avoid its logical tendency to oversimplify the matter by overlooking one of the two critical points involved. It will overstep the proper bounds and succumb to mass mechanisms on the one hand or elitism on the other.

Appendices

Introduction to the Series

FORMAT AND ORIGIN OF THIS SERIES

We have tried to make it easier for the reader to approach this series by using a coherent format. The essential aspects of our reflection on a given topic are contained in the initial article under each chapter. They are followed by a section entitled CLARIFICATIONS, in which we try to develop and apply more concretely the central lines of thought, to suggest study topics and related issues, and to go over one or more points in detail. Notes are given at the end of each of these two main divisions.

The notes are meant to be useful to the reader rather than to be erudite. Many of them are biblical, indicating other passages in Scripture which complement the thoughts presented or which can be used for related meditation. Instead of citing numerous scholarly works, we have limited ourselves to a few more accessible sources: e.g., the *Concilium* series. Our series was originally intended for a Latin American audience, and their needs were uppermost in our minds.

The type of theological reflection presented here can give rise to different discussion formats: full-length courses, study weeks, and the like. But we actually tested it in a seminar approach, involving intensive sessions of study, discussion, and prayer. It may interest the reader to know how our seminars actually operate.

As far as length of time is concerned, our experiences confirmed the feeling that the busy layman benefits more from short-term seminars in which he is actively involved than from long-term courses in which he is generally passive. So now we try to run seminars of three or four days that coincide with a holiday weekend. The aim is to provide five or six sessions of four hours each in a relatively short space of time. We also stress that enrollment in the seminar implies that the individual is willing to involve himself in it totally, to participate in all the sessions, and to remain until it is over. The seminar is meant to be a total experience, not mere attendance at a series of lectures.

Each four-hour session operates pretty much like this. It begins with a lecture (which is reproduced almost verbatim as the initial section of each chapter). The lecture lasts about one hour, and at its conclusion one or two questions are proposed to the various study groups (see Spring-board Questions in preceding volumes). But before they move into their discussion groups, the participants are asked to spend a few moments in personal meditation on the questions. In this way they can make an effort to formulate a personal solution, however provisional it might be, to the questions posed.

The various study groups then spend about forty-five minutes to an hour in discussing the questions. There are no more than ten persons in a given group, so that each individual will participate actively in the discussion. Herein lies the essential aim of the seminar itself, for the participants are supposed to move on from formulated truths to a truly interiorized truth. In other words, the discussion represents a confronta-tion between what they have heard and what they have learned from their real-life experiences; between that which they accepted uncritically as children and adolescents and that which they have put together into a coherent whole as adults.

Thus the questions proposed are not meant to serve as a review of the lecture material. They are meant to foster a great coherence between that which was provided in the lecture and other aspects or facts of Christian experience. To this end, it is highly desirable that the groups be somewhat heterogeneous in makeup, and that their discussion be stimulated by a pointed confrontation with things they may have read in the catechism or heard all their lives from the pulpit.

It is also highly useful at this point to have the groups make an effort to reach unanimity on their answers and then write them up as a group project. Such a procedure obliges the participants to engage in real dialogue and to respect differences of opinion. When this period is over, the various groups reassemble at a roundtable forum, and each group presents the answers it has formulated. The reply of the group may take one of three forms: a unanimous group response, a set of differing opinions, or a series of questions formulated by the group. It is our feeling that questions worked up by a group are more useful than those which an individual might formulate alone at the end of the lecture.

During the roundtable forum, the lecturer comments on the group replies, tries to respond to the questions of the various groups, and then takes up individual questions if he so desires.

The procedure varies for the final hour. Intellectual effort gives way to a period of prayer and recollection that is related to the theme under consideration. It may involve some form of paraliturgical service, or a biblical reading that is not discussed in great detail (see Appendix III in this volume).

This pattern is repeated throughout the course of the seminar. As circumstances permit, the final four-hour session may be dedicated to a review of what has been covered and a discussion of possible concrete applications in the local or parochial sector.

As the reader will see from the text itself, our aim is not to move on to a wholly different topic in each four-hour session. Experience has shown that it is more useful to return to the same few basic ideas over and over again, relating them ever more deeply to real-life problems. It is useful, in this connection, to sum up what has gone before at the start of each session. One practical way of doing this is to refer to conciliar texts that relate to the material in question (see Pertinent Conciliar Texts in preceding volumes). While we do not feel that these texts by themselves are enough to encourage this type of reflection, we do find that they are able to shore up and confirm the work already done. For they come from the Church gathered together in our day under the special action of the Holy Spirit.

Finally we would point out that this treatment of evolution and guilt has been preceded by a volume on the Church (Volume I), a volume on grace (Volume II), a volume on God (Volume III), and a volume on the sacraments (Volume IV). Each year a seminar is held on a new topic, and seminars on old topics are held for those who have not yet attended them. In this way we hope to answer the needs of mature persons who are looking for a theology which is equally adult, which is open to exploring new pathways related to their temporal commitments.

APPENDIX II

Distinctive Features of Volume Five

This final volume does not diverge fundamentally from the approach used in preparing the preceding four volumes. The theme was discussed and elaborated in conjunction with lay people. Seminars were held and intensive study sessions took place. But this fruitful experience taught us that the issues studies in this volume had certain distinctive features and imposed limitations of their own.

Our reflection on evolution and guilt breaks certain molds that were evident in the previous volumes. It does not deal so much with a central "dogma" of faith as with a certain mentality, a certain way of thinking, a particular method of analysis that can be applied to dogma and history.

The themes discussed in the previous volumes called up many memories: catechism lessons attended, sermons heard, and theoretical or practical formulas interwoven with Christian living. The earlier volumes sought to examine these past experiences, to put greater depth into them, or to correct them.

By contrast the topic "evolution" is practically virgin territory as far as Christian study and teaching is concerned. Moreover it is not a simple matter, despite the simplistic statements that are formulated about it in more or less intellectual circles. The evolutionary process and its dialectic are difficult problems with which the majority of today's Christians are unfamiliar.

On the other hand it seems impossible for Latin Americans to disregard it. Why? Because right now our continent is caught up in the task of shouldering greater and more active responsibility for an evolution that has so far proceeded without our active involvement and that has made us something we do not want to be. And is it not true that our passivity has been influenced to some extent by something that is in fact a Christian dogma: specifically, the notion of a sin located at the very start of human history, which provides an explanation and a justification for all our impotency?

A "theology for artisans of a new humanity" could not pass over this whole issue and its problems. But neither could it treat it in exactly the same way it treated the topics discussed in the previous volumes.

This accounts for some of the general features that are peculiar to this volume. It is more didactic and less dialogic than the preceding volumes. It cannot appeal as much to what the Christian already knows. Hence it must explain more and spell things out, moving at a pace that enables the reader to assimilate new categories.

The problems posed in the CLARIFCATIONS are not imaginary or hypothetical problems. They were not invented by the authors. They were experienced and posed by those who participated in the seminars. But to pose them precisely for the reader and offer the lineaments of a solution, we were forced to create a more methodical and broader work. Worst of all, it had to be more "academic."

What is more, the topic is vast in scope. Indeed it takes in everything and examines it in the light of evolution. Thus it may seem that we have scarcely touched upon the problems we present.

Because of our aims here, this volume also differs from the preceding ones in some of its concrete features. The individual chapters do not form neat units with their own list of Springboard Questions. Nor have we been able to provide Pertinent Conciliar Texts. The thought of Teilhard de Chardin certainly exerted a noticeable influence on Vatican II, particularly on its pastoral constitution *Gaudium et spes*. But even in that document we could not find passages which would expound or confirm the ideas expressed in the various chapters. Vatican II does not take up universal evolution *as a topic*, nor does it discuss how this process operates. Even our Biblical Tapestry here (Appendix III) is little more than a backdrop. While Scripture as a whole does provide a solid basis for an evolutionary interpretation, it was put together in the framework of an immobilist outlook, as we would logically expect, and its writers were completely unaware of the infinitely slow process that goes to make up divine creation.

Quite obviously all these remarks are directed to readers of the previous volumes, who expect to get more than a reading or lecture out of any given volume. Translating this reading or lecture into a concrete pastoral experience may demand more creativity in this case, as it did of us, and fewer prefabricated pedagogical devices.

But it is our conviction that the problematic discussed in this volume is a vital one for Christianity on our continent. For the time being it may reach fewer people and require greater education on their part. But their comprehension and circulation of this whole topic will determine the role that Christians will play in the liberation of Latin America and—why not?—their contribution to the positive evolution of humanity. We in our poverty, and precisely because we are poor, may have something new and worthwhile to say. That at least may serve as our excuse.

A Biblical Tapestry

When we read the Epistles of Saint Paul, and particularly when we read them in the light of the whole Old Testament, two things strike our attention almost immediately: the importance he attaches to history and what we could call his reinterpretation of sin. Deeply familiar with the Old Testament, Paul invites us to read it again with new eyes, to see it in the light cast by Jesus' revelation.

I Creation: Its Terminus and Its Obstacle

Saint Paul does not see God's creation as something in the past, as something that is over and done with. Indeed its final and definitive fate is not yet decided, because it is not independent of man's definitive destiny:

> The created universe waits with eager expectation for God's sons to be revealed. It was made the victim of frustration, not by its own choice, but because of him who made it so; yet always there was hope, because the universe itself is to be freed from the shackles of mortality and enter upon the liberty and splendour of the children of God (Rom. 8:19–21).

Thus the whole history of the universe is a gigantic pageant of liberation. Its goal is liberty, and this goal can only be achieved with the elimination of the frustration and destruction that affect what man wants to construct. Attaining that goal is an enormous, universal task:

> Up to the present, we know, the whole created universe groans in all its parts as if in the pangs of childbirth. Not only so, but even we, to whom the Spirit is given as firstfruits of the harvest to come, are groaning inwardly while we wait for God to make us his sons and set our whole body free (Rom. 8:22–23).

Creation is not finished. The function of creation is to pass from the hands of the Creator to the creative hands of man, as it were. In this way the liberty and creativity and splendor of the sons of God will be revealed. This suggests that we take another look at the divine message in the Old Testament and read it with greater depth.

1. **The message of creation in particular**: The very first account by the Yahwist writer shows us that God associates man with his creative work:

140

When the Lord God made earth and heaven, there was neither shrub nor plant growing wild upon the earth, because the Lord God had sent no rain on the earth; nor was there any man to till the ground. . . . Then the Lord God formed a man from the dust of the ground and breathed into his nostrils the breath of life. Thus the man became a living creature. Then the Lord God planted a garden in Eden away to the east, and there he put the man whom he had formed. . . . The Lord God took the man and put him in the garden of Eden to till it and care for it. . . . So God formed out of the ground all the wild animals and all the birds of heaven. He brought them to the man to see what he would call them, and whatever the man called each living creature, that was its name. Thus the man gave names to all cattle, to the birds of heaven, and to every wild animal (Gen. 2:5–8,15,19–20).

The priestly account, composed some time later, presents the same message in its more developed but less imaginative form:

Then God said, 'Let us make man in our image and likeness to rule the fish in the sea, the birds of heaven, the cattle, all wild animals on earth, and all reptiles that crawl upon the earth.' So God created man in his own image; in the image of God he created him; male and female he created them. God blessed them and said to them, 'Be fruitful and increase, fill the earth and subdue it' (Gen. 1:26–28).

2. **But why doesn't this take place automatically**? Why does it turn into a slow and difficult road? Why does it become a task in history? Why is it that the creatures man named will not obey him? Here again the Yahwist writer offers us the first explanation:

And to the man he said [after the sin]: 'Because you . . . have eaten from the tree which I forbade you, accursed shall be the ground on your account. With labor you shall win your food from it all the days of your life. It will grow thorns and thistles for you . . . You shall gain your bread by the sweat of your brow until you return to the ground; for from it you were taken. Dust you are, to dust you shall return.'. . . The Lord God . . . said, 'The man has become like one of us, knowing good and evil' (Gen. 3:17–19,21–22).

That is why man, who was supposed to subdue the earth to himself, subdued it to frustration. That is why the earth groans, waiting for man's liberation. This is also evident in the enslavement generated by one of the elements that was created by God and is in his likeness insofar as it is creative: sexuality:

To the woman he said: 'I will increase your labour and your groaning, and in labour you shall bear children. You shall be eager for your husband, and he shall be your master' (Gen. 3:16).

The Book of Wisdom, composed near the end of the Old Testament period, picks up this theme once again: history really starts with an alienated liberty. Fundamentally it is marked by death. Only redemption from the body, for which we long, will make us creative:

God created man for immortality, and made him the image of his own
eternal self; it was the devil's spite that brought death into the world (Wis.
2:23–24).

Liberty, then, opens up as a future prospect. God's creative Wisdom

kept guard over the first father of the human race, when he alone had yet
been made; she saved him after his fall, and gave him the strength to
master all things (Wis. 10:1–2).

II The Pathway: The Revelation of Sin

So we have the original situation, enslavement, and the final situation,
creative liberty. The obstacle is not transgressions of the law. It is Sin
with a capital: i.e., liberty paralyzed by desire and death. God's activity in
history, in which man progressively collaborates, is to give full meaning
to creation with the liberation (redemption) of man. But how will this be
achieved? Saint Paul conceives two stages, which are to take place in the
course of time but which are also reproduced in our own lives: *the revelation of sin and the revelation of grace.*

As we have seen, the original situation of man starting with Adam is
the reign of sin. In other words, it is a condition of enslavement and
death. But no precise law condemns man:

It was through one man that sin entered the world, and through sin death,
and thus death pervaded the whole human race, inasmuch as all men have
sinned. For sin was already in the world before there was law, though in
the absence of law no reckoning is kept of sin. But death held sway from
Adam to Moses, even over those who had not sinned as Adam did, by
disobeying a direct command (Rom. 5:12–14).

Thus there is a sin that affects all human beings. But there are two different ways of being enslaved to it. One is total, the other is filled with
anguish but closer to salvation. And it is the law that divides the
two ways:

We have already drawn up the accusation that Jews and Greeks alike are
all under the power of sin. This has scriptural warrant: 'There is no just
man, not one; no one who understands, no one who seeks God. All have
swerved aside, all alike have become debased; there is no one to show
kindness; no, not one . . . ' Now all the words of the law are addressed, as
we know, to those who are within the pale of the law, so that no one may
have anything to say in self-defence, but the whole world may be exposed
to the judgment of God. For (again from Scripture) 'no human being can
be justified in the sight of God' for having kept the law: law brings only the
consciousness of sin (Rom. 3:9–12,19–20).

This is how Paul describes the reality of each and every human being:

We know that the law is spiritual; but I am not: I am unspiritual, the
purchased slave of sin. I do not even acknowledge my own actions as mine,
for what I do is not what I want to do, but what I detest. . . . I discover this
principle, then: that when I want to do the right, only the wrong is within

my reach. In my inmost self I delight in the law of God, but I perceive that there is in my bodily members a different law, fighting against the law that my reason approves and making me a prisoner under the law that is in my members, the law of sin (Rom. 7:14–15,21–23).

Discovering this fact is a decisive experience in the liberation of man. And for that it is necessary that sin, which lies dormant and diffuse in our everyday activity, reveal its force and power. We must experience death and thus prepare our resurrection to liberty:

In the absence of law, sin is a dead thing. There was a time when, in the absence of law, I was fully alive [apparently]: but when the commandment came, sin sprang to life and I died (Rom. 7:8–9).

As Saint Paul sees it, this experience reveals the Spirit and is the Spirit's work. Why? Because the danger is not a consciously noted death. The danger lies in the infantilism of a death that is felt to be life, and an enslavement that does now know it is enslavement:

Then what of the law? It was added to make wrongdoing a legal offence (Gal. 3:19).*

This conscious encounter with the borderline-limit of the human condition and man's dying to it is the first step toward creative liberty:

It follows, my friends, that our lower nature has no claim upon us; we are not obliged to live on that level. If you do so, you must die. But if by the Spirit you put to death all the base pursuits of the body, then you will live (Rom. 8:12–13).

As we mentioned earlier, Paul's teaching directs us back to God's revelation in the Old Testament. His statement that the law merely makes us conscious of being sinners offers a new way of interpreting important aspects of what was called "the law" and what in fact was a *history*. In particular, it enables us to glimpse the significance of two parallel lives in Israel: the life of Saul and the life of David.

1. **The history of Saul and of David,** the first two lay kings of Yahweh's anointed people, begins with a sin as all human history does. (This is true at least in the tradition of the prophets and Deuteronomy):

They said to Samuel, 'Pray for us your servants to the Lord your God, to save us from death; for we have added to all our other sins the great wickedness of asking for a king.' Samuel said to the people, 'Do not be afraid; although you have been so wicked, do not give up the worship of the Lord, but serve him with all your heart' (1 Sam. 12:19–20).

Sin is not something that has to be erased, so that one can start over again with a fresh, clean slate. God will build up the history of Israel on the foundation of this sin. But it seems that Saul lives out his whole life

*See the exegesis of this text by Stanislas Lyonnet in *The Christian Lives by the Spirit,* Eng. trans. (New York: Alba House, 1972).

under the unconscious weight of this sinful guilt. His reign has scarcely begun when it appears to be falsified by the latent tension between his duties as king and the religious realm:

> Some of them crossed the Jordan into the district of Gad and Gilead, but Saul remained at Gilgal, and all the people at his back were in alarm. He waited seven days for his meeting with Samuel, but Samuel did not come to Gilgal; so the people began to drift away from Saul. He said therefore, 'Bring me the whole-offering and the shared-offerings', and he offered up the whole-offering. Saul had just finished the sacrifice, when Samuel arrived, and he went out to greet him. Samuel said, 'What have you done' (1 Sam. 13:7–10).

Saul, a sinner like any other sinner, is caught in the same situation that any sinner is. He does not consciously and freely shoulder his action before Yahweh in order to confirm it or beg pardon for it. He vacillates, swayed by his latent guiltiness:

> Saul answered 'I saw that the people were drifting away from me, and you yourself had not come as you had promised, and the Philistines were assembling at Michmash; and I thought, "The Philistines will now move against me at Gilgal, and I have not placated the Lord"; so I felt *compelled* to make the whole-offering myself.' Samuel said to Saul, 'You have behaved foolishly' (1 Sam. 13:11–13).

Note the words. Saul is "compelled" and "foolish," not exactly a "sinner." David will do things that are a thousand times more serious, but he will not be "foolish" or "compelled." The narrative tells another story along these same lines, indicating that Saul lacked something in humanity, audacity, and clear-sightedness. (These qualities seem to enter into account wherever liberation is concerned, even up to and beyond the point of sin):

> The Lord delivered Israel that day, and the fighting passed on beyond Beth-aven. Now the Israelites on that day had been driven to exhaustion. Saul had adjured the people in these words: 'A curse be on the man who eats any food before nightfall . . . ' So no one ate any food. Now there was honeycomb in the country-side; but when his men came upon it, dripping with honey though it was, not one of them put his hand to his mouth, for fear of the oath. But Jonathan had not heard his father lay this solemn prohibition on the people, and he stretched out the stick that was in his hand, dipped the end of it in the honeycomb, put it to his mouth and was refreshed. One of the people said to him, 'Your father solemnly forbade this; he said, "A curse on the man who eats food today!"' Now the men were faint with hunger. Jonathan said, 'My father has done the people nothing but harm; see how I am refreshed by this mere taste of honey. How much better if the people had eaten today whatever they took from their enemies by way of spoil! Then there would indeed have been a great slaughter of Philistines' (1 Sam. 14:23–30).

There is no doubt that the sacred author approves of Jonathan's action. But once again Saul is weighed down by his latent guiltiness and fear. He follows the letter of the law and denies his personal feelings as a father, believing that he will thereby placate Yahweh:

> Saul said to Jonathan, 'Tell me what you have done.' Jonathan told him, 'True, I did taste a little honey on the tip of my stick. Here I am; I am ready to die.' Then Saul swore a great oath that Jonathan should die. But the people said to Saul, 'Shall Jonathan die, Jonathan who has won this great victory for Israel? God forbid! As the Lord lives, not a hair of his head shall fall to the ground, for he has been at work with God today.' So the people ransomed Jonathan and he did not die (1 Sam. 14:43–45).

Not surpisingly, then, at the end of his history Saul is presented as a man possessed, that is, a man who is not free. On the one hand his fear of the Lord may prevent him from committing great crimes; David committed greater ones. But on the other hand it makes him incapable of a sin that is openly recognized as such, and hence of personal maturity. He appears to exemplify an infantile fear of liberty:

> Next day an evil spirit from God seized upon Saul; he fell into a frenzy in the house, and David played the harp to him as he had before. Saul had his spear in his hand, and he hurled it at David, meaning to pin him to the wall; but twice David swerved aside. After this Saul was afraid of David, because he saw that the Lord had forsaken him and was with David. He therefore removed David from his household and appointed him to the command of a thousand men (1 Sam. 18:10–13).

The final picture of Saul is a picture of childish anxiety looking to its parent (Samuel in this case) as an escape from liberty:

> Saul put on different clothes and went in disguise with two of his men. He came to the woman by night and said, 'Tell me my fortunes by consulting the dead, and call up the man I name to you.' . . . The woman answered, 'I see a ghostly form . . . like an old man coming up, wrapped in a cloak.' Then Saul knew it was Samuel, and he bowed low with his face to the ground, and prostrated himself. Samuel said to Saul, 'Why have you disturbed me and brought me up?' Saul answered, 'I am in great trouble; the Philistines are pressing me and God has turned away; he no longer answers me through prophets or through dreams, and I have summoned you to tell me what I should do' (1 Sam. 28:8,13–15).

Perhaps the whole key to the story of Saul and his life is to be found in what Saint Paul says of the Israelites in general: "Israel made great efforts after a law of righteousness, but never attained to it. Why was this? Because their efforts were not based on faith, but (as they supposed) on deeds" (Rom. 9:31–32).

2. **The history of David** is practically the counterpoint to the history of Saul. Saul is rejected and set aside. David is put in his place because he has a characteristic that is thoroughly pleasing to God:

> Samuel said to Saul, 'You have behaved foolishly . . . Now your line will not endure; the Lord will seek a man after his own heart, and will appoint him prince over his people . . . ' (1 Sam. 13:13–14).

How does this man "after his own heart" act? Jesus himself describes him as a man liberated from fear of God, as a man who does "what was not permitted" and acts rightly in so doing. Why? Because he exercises a liberty that has been given to man and that Saul did not dare to use at Gilgal:

> Have you never read what David did when he and his men were hungry and had nothing to eat? He went into the House of God,. in the time of Abiathar the High Priest, and ate the sacred bread though no one but a priest is allowed to eat it, and even gave it to his men . . . The Sabbath was made for the sake of man and not man for the Sabbath (Mark. 2:25–27).

This free man "after God's own heart" experiences a revelation of what sin is. The sin in question is his sin with Bathsheba, the wife of Uriah. It is little more than a passing impulse, but it will set in motion an intricate interplay of persons:

> She conceived, and sent word to David that she was pregnant. David ordered Joab to send Uriah [who is away at war] the Hittite to him (2 Sam. 11:5–6).

Now there begins a lying game designed to throw the paternity of the child on Uriah. But David finds himself faced with a person, a whole person:

> David heard that Uriah had not gone home, and said to him, 'You have had a long journey, why did you not go home?' Uriah answered David, 'Israel and Judah are under canvas, and so is the Ark, and my lord Joab and your majesty's officers are camping in the open; how can I go home to eat and drink and to sleep with my wife? By your life, I cannot do this!' . . . The following morning David wrote a letter to Joab and *sent Uriah with it*. He wrote in the letter, 'Put Uriah opposite the enemy where the fighting is fiercest and then fall back, and leave him to meet his death' (2 Sam. 11:10–15).

The plot is carried out and it works. Uriah dies:

> When Uriah's wife heard that her husband was dead, she mourned for him; and when the period of mourning was over, David sent for her and brought her into his house. She became his wife and bore him a son. But what David had done was wrong in the eyes of the Lord (2 Sam. 11:26–27).

It is precisely at this point that the revelation of sin will come to David. But why precisely is David the type of person who is capable of receiving this revelation? We could put it this way. He is capable of receiving it because he has situated his whole life on the plane of personal relationships, because he has freed himself in large measure from the type of fear that falsified and depersonalized Saul's reactions. Compare Saul's reaction to Jonathan's honey-tasting with this reaction of David's:

> At that time David was in the stronghold and a Philistine garrison held Bethlehem. One day a longing came over David, and he exclaimed, 'If only I could have a drink of water from the well by the gate of Bethlehem!' At

this the heroic three made their way through the Philistine lines and drew water from the well by the gate of Bethlehem and brought to David. But David refused to drink it; he poured it out to the Lord and said, 'God forbid that I should do such a thing! Can I drink the blood of these men who risked their lives for it?' (2 Sam. 23:14–17).

This is the value that David saw in human beings. When he looked at a human being he saw a person. And it is to such a person that God will reveal what sin is through the *Law*. But the law here is not a cold-blooded precept. It is a comparison made by a prophet that will show up the evil deed in its true light:

The Lord sent Nathan the prophet to David, and when he entered his presence, he said to him, 'There were once two men in the same city, one rich and the other poor. The rich man had flocks and herds, but the poor man had nothing of his own except one little ewe lamb. He reared it himself, and it grew up in his home with his own sons. It ate from his dish, drank from his cup and nestled in his arms; it was like a daughter to him. One day a traveller came to the rich man's house, and he, too mean to take something from his own flocks and herds to serve to his guest, took the poor man's lamb and served up that.' David was very angry, and burst out, 'As the Lord lives, the man who did this deserves to die . . . ' Then Nathan said to David, 'You are the man. . . . You have struck down Uriah the Hittite with the sword . . . and you have stolen his wife . . . ' David said to Nathan, 'I have sinned against the Lord.' Nathan answered him, 'The Lord has laid on another the consequences of your sin . . . ' (2 Sam. 12:1–13).

It almost seems as if it does not really bother God that David sins, because God is aware of David's faith and personal trust and uprightness. He knows that David will come to appreciate his sin and will return to his place in God's heart. And so we get this singular episode:

Once again the Israelites felt the Lord's anger, when he incited David against them and gave him orders that Israel and Judah should be counted. . . . After he had counted the people David's conscience smote him, and he said to the Lord, 'I have done a very wicked thing: I pray thee, Lord, remove thy servant's guilt, for I have been very foolish.' He rose next morning, and meanwhile the command of the Lord had come to the prophet Gad, David's seer, to go and speak to David: 'This is the word of the Lord: I have three things in store for you; choose one and I will bring it upon you . . . Is it to be three years of famine in your land, or three months of flight with the enemy at your heels, or three days of pestilence in your land? Consider carefully what answer I am to take back to him who sent me.' Thereupon David said to Gad, 'I am in a desperate plight; let us fall into the hands of the Lord, for his mercy is great . . . ' So the Lord sent a pestilence throughout Israel. . . . When David saw the angel who was striking down the people, he said to the Lord, 'It is I who have done wrong, the sin is mine; but these poor sheep, what have they done? Let thy hand fall upon me and upon my family' (2 Sam. 24:1–17).

Again we can use the words of Saint Paul to sum up our picture of this great figure in Israel, for they seem to apply to every stage of his life: "Law intruded into this process to multiply law-breaking. But where sin was thus multiplied, grace immeasurably exceeded it" (Rom. 5:20–21).

And the reason is that the law, when properly interpreted (as Paul would demand), pointed out what sin really was: the denial of the personal element. Raised to that level, sin itself is transformed into a wellspring of goodness insofar as it throws man into the personal arms of God and the fraternal arms of his fellowmen—as it did in the case of David.